Disclaimer

This book contains fictionalized names, scenarios, and examples used for illustrative purposes only. Any resemblance to actual persons, living or dead, or actual events is purely coincidental.

The information presented herein is intended for educational and informational purposes. It reflects the author's research, experiences, and opinions as of the publication date. It is not intended as a substitute for professional advice, including but not limited to medical, legal, financial, or psychological counsel.

While the author and publisher have made reasonable efforts to ensure the accuracy and completeness of the information, due to the evolving nature of research and the potential for human error, no guarantees are made regarding its absolute accuracy, completeness, or timeliness.

Readers are advised to consult with qualified professionals for advice tailored to their specific circumstances. The author and publisher disclaim any liability for errors, omissions, or actions taken based on the information provided in this book.

Dedication

To the dreamers, the doers, and the bold movers who shape the world of tomorrow.

To Gen Z-your energy, ambition, and limitless potential inspired every word of this book. You are redefining success, breaking boundaries, and leading with courage in ways the world has never seen.

May this book guide you in making bold moves with courage, resilience, and authenticity.

CONTENTS

PART 3

PART 4

THE INSPIRATION FOR *BOLD MOVES*

Navigating the professional world can feel like charting unknown territory. Technical skills are important, but what I have learned throughout my career is that it is the *intangibles* – your mindset, resilience, and ability to connect with people – that truly set you apart. That's why I wrote *BOLD MOVES: Redefining Soft Skills for Gen Z and Beyond*. This book is for everyone—regardless of their specific role—who wants to thrive in today's challenging work environment.

I authored this book because I want to empower professionals, especially Gen Z, to build the mental and emotional strength they need for lasting success. So many talented Gen Z professionals struggle to transition from campus to career. They might stumble out of the gate, find it hard to settle in, or struggle to connect with colleagues, clients, or managers. The professional world can be daunting, whether you're working in a big corporation, a small startup, a hospital, a construction site, or anywhere in between. Imposter syndrome, fear of failure, and a lack of direction can hold you back. I've seen it happen. But I've also seen people, even those facing huge challenges, achieve amazing things by embracing a growth mindset and taking deliberate action.

My own journey has taught me that success isn't just about tackling technical challenges; it's about mastering how we connect, communicate, collaborate, and lead. *BOLD MOVES* is my way of sharing these insights in a practical, accessible way, so you can navigate your career with confidence and resilience.

This book is designed to help you develop the essential skills that will form the foundation of your success. These skills will help you stand out from the crowd and lead effectively, collaborate seamlessly, and adapt quickly to change. Whether you're just starting out or looking to level up your career, this book offers practical tools, frameworks, and inspiration.

Part 1, *Standing Out*, is all about making your mark. We'll explore the power of communication, building your personal brand, and the art of storytelling. Part 2, *Leading Strong*, focuses on cultivating leadership qualities that build trust, inspire others, and foster collaboration in diverse teams. Finally, in Part 3, *Staying Resilient*, we dive into the mindsets and techniques needed to thrive in a world of constant change, manage your time effectively, and bounce back from setbacks.

I truly believe that with the right mindset and a dedication to growth, *anyone* can overcome obstacles and unlock their full potential. I hope that *BOLD MOVES* will ignite your passion, sharpen your focus, and boost your confidence as you pursue your career – just as these principles have guided me.

Welcome to a journey of career transformation, where technical know-how meets emotional intelligence, where communication builds genuine connections, and where resilience becomes your superpower in today's dynamic world of work.

I hope this book becomes your trusted companion on the road to success. The path ahead might have its bumps, but with the right mindset, skills, and strategies, you can make bold moves that will redefine your career and your life. Let's get started!

Introduction

In a world that's constantly shifting under the weight of innovation and change, the game's rules have been rewritten. Once, success was built on the foundation of technical expertise and a linear career trajectory. But today, in a workplace dominated by collaboration, rapid technological advancements, and global interconnectivity, it's not just about what you know—it's about how you navigate the unknown.

Welcome to the era of bold moves.

If you're part of Gen Z, you already know the workplace you're stepping into is unlike any other. You're entering a space where hierarchies are flattening, careers look more like lattices than ladders, and success requires more than just doing the job. It demands adaptability, emotional intelligence, and a unique ability to connect with others—skills that aren't always taught but are always noticed.

And this book is here to help.

In Bold Moves: Redefining Soft Skills for Gen Z and Beyond, we'll explore the ten essential soft skills that will not only help you thrive in this ever-evolving world but also set you apart as a leader, a collaborator, and a trailblazer. From mastering the art of communication to building resilience in the face of setbacks, each chapter is a deep dive into the practical skills you need to claim your space and make your mark.

But this isn't just a book about skills; it's a call to action. It's an invitation to step out of your comfort zone, to challenge the status quo, and to redefine what it means to be successful in the modern workplace. The truth is, soft skills aren't soft at all—they're the hard currency of today's professional world, and learning to wield them is your superpower.

Whether you're just starting your career, pivoting to a new opportunity, or striving to lead with impact, this book will equip you with the tools and insights you need to take control of your journey. The workplace of tomorrow belongs to those who can think boldly, act decisively, and connect authentically. And that starts with redefining what it means to be skilled.

So, are you ready to make your bold move? Let's dive in.

THE DIFFERENT GENERATIONS WE NEED TO KNOW

Understanding the different generations is important because they have distinct characteristics, values, and experiences that shape their perspectives and behaviors. Here's a breakdown of the main generations you should know:

Traditionalists or the Silent Generation (born 1928-1945): Shaped by the Great Depression, World War II, and post-war prosperity, they are respectful of authority, loyal, disciplined, hardworking, and thrifty.

Baby Boomers (born 1946-1964): Shaped by the post-war economic boom, civil rights movement, Vietnam War, and social/political change, they are optimistic, competitive, individualistic, work-centric, and value personal and financial success.

Generation X (born 1965-1980): Shaped by economic uncertainty, being "latchkey kids", the rise of MTV and personal computers, they are independent, resourceful, self-reliant, skeptical, and value work-life balance.

Millennials or Generation Y (born 1981-1996): Shaped by the digital revolution, 9/11, the Great Recession, and social media, they are tech-savvy, collaborative, purpose-driven, value experiences, and seek work-life integration.

Generation Z (born 1997-2010): Shaped by growing up with technology and social media, economic instability, and increased diversity, Generation Z is a digital native, entrepreneurial, innovative, values authenticity, and seeks meaningful work.

Generation Alpha (born 2011-2024): Shaped by growing up in a world dominated by technology and social media, with increased awareness of social and environmental issues, they are highly tech-dependent, diverse, creative, and adaptable.

Generation Beta (born 2025-2039): They will grow up surrounded by advanced technology like AI, autonomous vehicles, and virtual reality. This generation is likely to be highly conscious of environmental issues, shape new norms focused on sustainability and innovation, and fully experience the 21st century's tech advancements.

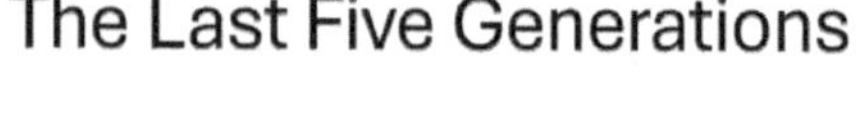

The Last Five Generations

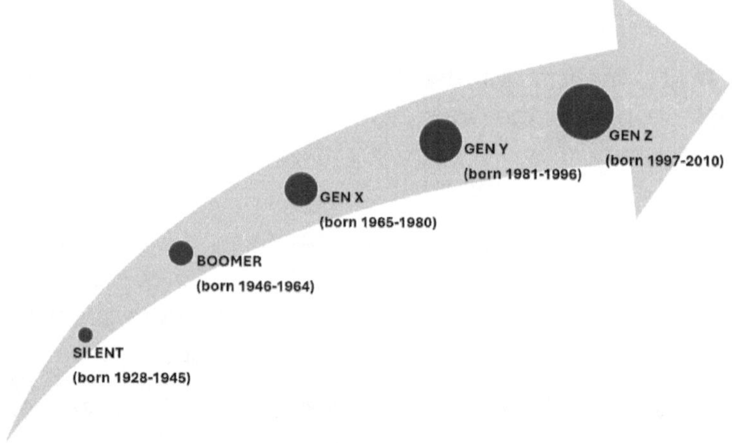

Why does it matter?

Understanding generational differences can help us to:

- Improve communication and collaboration, as different generations have different communication styles and preferences.

- Manage and motivate employees effectively, as each generation has unique values and motivators in the workplace.

♦ Market products and services more effectively, as understanding generational needs and preferences is crucial for successful marketing.

♦ Bridge generational gaps by recognizing and appreciating the strengths and perspectives of different generations, fostering greater understanding and respect.

Keep in mind that these are generalizations, and individuals within each generation can vary widely. However, understanding these broad trends can offer valuable insights into how different generations interact with the world around them.

Navigating Today's Workplace: Gen Z Challenges

Generation Z professionals are entering a work landscape vastly different from previous generations. Shaped by the digital age, they bring unique strengths and face distinct challenges. Understanding these dynamics is crucial for both their success and the evolution of modern workplaces. Gen Z desires meaningful work that aligns with their values. However, they often encounter a gig economy with less stable employment and fewer traditional career paths, making finding purpose-driven work challenging. They also struggle to find companies whose values align with their own. As digital natives, Gen Z is comfortable with technology, but they also experience digital fatigue. They crave authentic connections and struggle with the pressure of constant online presence and communication. The need to maintain a strong online presence for professional reasons creates added stress.

Gen Z prioritizes mental health, but they face increased stress due to economic uncertainty, social pressures, and the blurring of work-life boundaries. The constant need to be available, due to technology, makes it difficult to maintain a healthy work-life balance. While they value collaboration, remote work and digital communication can make it difficult to build strong team relationships and foster a sense of belonging. The lack of in-person interaction can make it difficult to build strong professional networks. Gen Z thrives on immediate feedback and expects rapid career development. However, traditional workplaces may not offer the speed or frequency of feedback they desire. They must learn how to advocate for their own development and how to receive and implement feedback.

Gen Z seeks transparent and collaborative leadership, but they may encounter traditional hierarchical structures that don't meet their expectations. They must learn to navigate different leadership styles and to influence change from within organizations. In essence, Gen Z professionals are tasked with finding purpose, balance, and connection in a rapidly changing work environment. Their ability to adapt, advocate for their needs, and leverage their digital skills will shape their success.

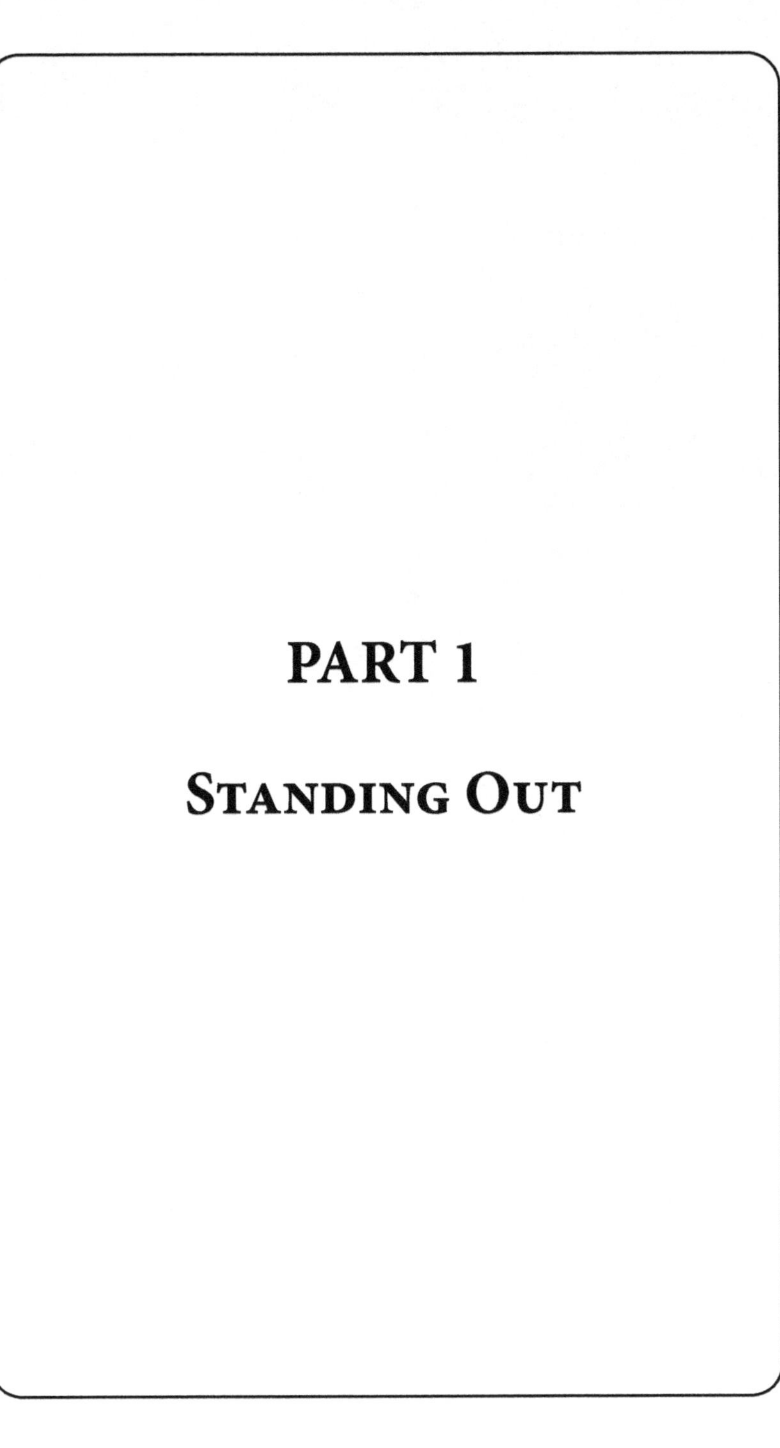

PART 1

STANDING OUT

Chapter 1

MASTERING DIGITAL COMMUNICATION: SPEAKING HUMAN IN A DIGITAL WORLD

In today's hyper-connected world, where emojis replace expressions and GIFs kick-start conversations, digital communication is more important than ever. While technology makes connecting easier, it also brings new challenges—messages can be misinterpreted, tone gets lost, and genuine human connection is harder to maintain. Mastering digital communication is not just about typing fast or using the latest tools but about building real, meaningful online interactions.

Emails, DMs, video calls, and instant messages have replaced face-to-face conversations. While these tools make communication faster and more convenient, they also raise questions: How do you express tone in a text? Build trust on a Zoom call? Understand cultural differences when emojis do the talking? This is where Peter Drucker's insight becomes crucial: "The most important thing in communication is hearing what isn't said." In the digital realm, where non-verbal cues are often absent, we must actively seek to understand the unspoken—the nuances behind the emojis, the pauses in a video call, and the implied meanings in a text. Digital communication is not just a skill—it's the foundation of how we work, collaborate, and connect. But it takes more than just hitting "send" to get it right. It requires thoughtfulness, empathy, and an awareness of how your words (or silence) impact others, demanding that we 'hear' what is left unsaid.

In this chapter, we will explore how to communicate clearly and authentically in the digital space. You will learn how to craft messages that stand out, avoid common mistakes, and foster genuine connections—even from miles away. Whether you are leading a remote team, networking across time zones, or trying to make your email matter, this chapter will give you the tools to communicate with confidence and impact.

The digital world moves fast, but the key to effective communication remains the same—it's about the person, not the platform. Let's dive in and learn how to bring your best self to every digital conversation.

Digital Empathy: The Heart of Human Connection Online

In the absence of face-to-face interaction, digital empathy becomes paramount. It's the ability to understand and respond to the emotions of others through the written word, video calls, or even a simple chat message.

- **Decoding Digital Cues:** Body language and tone of voice are often absent in digital communication. This makes careful word choice and consideration of the recipient's perspective essential. Think about the impact of a curt "Okay" versus a more engaged "Sounds good, thanks!" The latter conveys warmth and acknowledges the other person's contribution.

- **The Power of Personalization:** Generic messages often fall flat. Personalization, like using someone's name, referencing a shared experience, or acknowledging their recent work, can transform a routine interaction into a meaningful exchange. A LinkedIn message that starts with "Hi [Name], I was impressed by your recent article on [Topic]..." is far more likely to get a response than a generic connection request.

- **Context is King:** Before sending any message, consider the recipient's context. Are they likely to be busy? Stressed? Understanding their potential state of mind can help you tailor your message for maximum impact.

The Rise of "Zoom Fatigue" and the Importance of Human-Centered Digital Communication

In early 2020, as the COVID-19 pandemic forced millions of people to work and socialize from home, one of the most significant changes was the rise of video conferencing platforms, like Zoom. While these platforms allowed people to continue working, learning, and connecting despite social distancing, they also introduced a new phenomenon: Zoom fatigue.

For many people, virtual meetings became the norm, but over time, people began to experience burnout. This was not just about spending long hours in front of a screen; it was about the lack of natural human cues and connection. As virtual meetings grew more frequent, people began to feel increasingly disconnected, exhausted, and disengaged.

One particular story stood out—a manager at a global company, who had been hosting numerous back-to-back virtual meetings, noticed that team morale was dropping. Despite being in constant digital communication, his team felt more isolated than ever. He decided to change his approach. Instead of running meetings with the usual rigid structure of agenda items and productivity-focused goals, he began to start each meeting with a personal check-in—asking each person how they were feeling or about something they enjoyed that week. He even took a few minutes to acknowledge their challenges and offer words of encouragement.

This minor change in digital communication had a profound effect. The team felt more connected and supported, and their productivity improved. By simply speaking human in a digital environment—acknowledging the emotional and personal well-being of his team—the manager built a stronger, more cohesive work environment, even remotely.

This story demonstrates that while digital tools can make communication more convenient, they can also feel sterile and disconnected. To truly master digital communication, we need to prioritize human connection. Whether through a simple greeting, understanding emotions, or showing empathy, speaking human means recognizing the person behind the screen and fostering meaningful interactions, even in a virtual space.

Digital communication tools are powerful, but they can't replace the human element. To truly connect in a digital world, we need to center our communication around empathy, connection, and understanding. Making room for personal connection and emotional well-being in digital environments helps us maintain stronger relationships, even when we're miles apart.

Navigating the Nuances of Digital Expression

Digital communication is rife with potential for misinterpretation. Understanding these nuances is crucial for effective communication.

- **The Emoji Enigma:** Emojis can add personality and emotion to digital conversations, but their meaning can be subjective and culturally dependent. A thumbs-up emoji, while generally positive, can be perceived as dismissive in some contexts. Over-reliance on emojis can also appear unprofessional. Use them judiciously and always prioritize clarity.

- **GIFs and Memes:** A Double-Edged Sword: GIFs and memes can be a fun way to express yourself, but they can also be confusing or inappropriate in professional settings. Consider your audience and the context before using them.

- **Digital Shorthand and Slang:** Tread Carefully: While slang and abbreviations are common in casual online interactions, they can create barriers in professional communication. Avoid jargon and technical terms unless you're certain your audience understands them. When in doubt, err on the side of formality and clarity.

- **Tone in Text:** A Delicate Balance: Conveying tone in written communication can be challenging. A message that seems perfectly polite to you might be interpreted differently by the recipient. Read your messages aloud before sending them to ensure they convey the intended tone.

Communication That Connects: Building Bridges, Not Walls

Effective communication is about more than just transmitting information; it's about building relationships and fostering understanding.

- **Active Listening in the Digital Age:** Active listening isn't limited to face-to-face conversations. In digital spaces, it involves carefully reading and considering the other person's message, asking clarifying questions, and acknowledging their perspective. Even a simple "Thanks for sharing that, I understand your point" can go a long way in building rapport.

- **Expressing Ideas with Clarity and Conciseness:** Avoid rambling or overly complex sentences. Get to the point quickly and clearly, especially in written communication. Use bullet points, headings, and short paragraphs to make your messages easier to digest.

- **The Art of Digital Storytelling:** Storytelling is a powerful tool for engaging your audience and making your message memorable. Even in digital communication, you can weave narratives into your emails, presentations, and social media posts to connect with your audience on an emotional level.

- **Feedback:** The Fuel for Growth: Be open to receiving feedback on your communication style. Ask colleagues or mentors for their perspective on how you can improve. Constructive criticism can be invaluable for honing your communication skills.

Mastering Digital Communication Channels: Choosing the Right Tool for the Job

Different communication channels serve different purposes. Understanding the strengths and weaknesses of each platform is essential for effective communication.

- **Email:** The Professional Staple: Email is still a cornerstone of professional communication. Craft clear and concise subject lines, structure your emails logically, and always proofread before sending.

- **Video Conferencing:** Bridging the Distance: Video calls offer a more personal connection than email or instant messaging. Maintain eye contact with the camera, pay attention to your body language, and create a professional environment for virtual meetings.

- **Instant Messaging:** The Speed of Now: Instant messaging platforms like Slack and Microsoft Teams are ideal for quick questions, informal updates, and collaborative discussions. However, avoid using them for complex or sensitive conversations.

- **Social Media:** Building Your Personal Brand: Social media platforms offer a powerful way to build your personal brand and connect with others in your field. Be mindful of your online presence and curate a professional image.

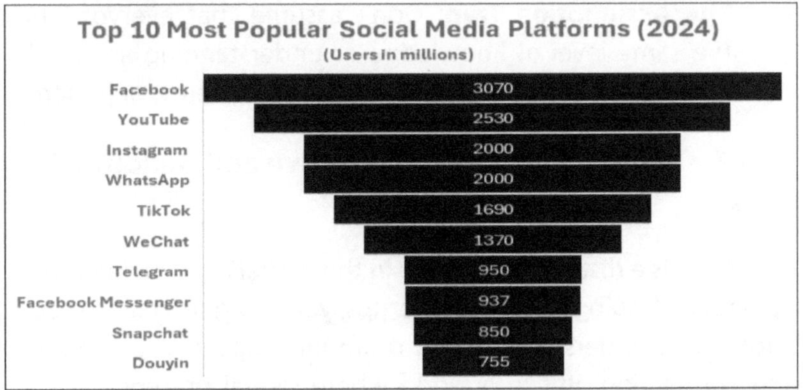

Avoiding Common Pitfalls: Navigating the Digital Minefield

Digital communication is full of potential pitfalls. Being aware of these traps can help you avoid misunderstandings and maintain positive relationships.

- **The Perils of Tone Misinterpretation:** As mentioned earlier, conveying tone in text can be challenging. Be mindful of how your words might be interpreted and add context where necessary.

- **The Over-Communication Trap:** Bombarding people with unnecessary emails or messages can lead to information overload and resentment. Be selective about what you communicate and avoid sending unnecessary updates.

- **The Under-Communication Trap:** Failing to share critical information can be equally problematic. Ensure that your team and stakeholders are kept informed of important developments.

- **The Timing Trap:** Sending messages outside of working hours can disrupt work-life balance and create a sense of pressure. Respect boundaries and schedule messages for appropriate times.

- **The Assumption Trap:** Don't assume that everyone has the same level of knowledge or understanding as you do. Provide context and explain any technical terms or jargon.

Gen Z: Owning Your Digital Narrative and Building Your Tribe

Gen Z holds a distinct advantage in the digital age. Having grown up with technology at your fingertips, you navigate online spaces effortlessly, understanding the profound impact of community and connection. But in a world where digital presence shapes personal and professional opportunities, mastering digital communication goes beyond just being active online—it's about being intentional, authentic, and strategic.

- **Crafting Your Digital Identity:** Your online presence is your digital resume, a reflection of your skills, passions, and values. Thoughtfully curating your content ensures that your digital footprint aligns with your aspirations and personal brand.

- **Building Meaningful Connections:** Engaging in industry conversations, networking with like-minded individuals, and participating in relevant digital communities can open doors to new opportunities. Genuine interactions foster long-term relationships.

- **Content Creation:** Sharing Your Expertise: Sharing valuable insights through blogs, articles, videos, or social media helps position you as a thought leader. By offering knowledge and perspectives, you contribute to the collective digital discourse.

- **Collaboration in the Digital Age:** Digital collaboration tools enable seamless teamwork across distances. Leveraging these tools effectively allows you to contribute to shared projects, work with global teams, and enhance productivity.

The Story of "Humans of New York" and the Power of Empathy

In 2010, Brandon Stanton, a former bond trader, embarked on a photography project that would transform digital storytelling. His idea was simple: capture portraits of everyday New Yorkers and pair them with short narratives. What began as a personal endeavor soon evolved into *Humans of New York (HONY)*—a global storytelling phenomenon demonstrating authenticity's extraordinary power in digital communication.

Stanton's success was not just about photography; it was about human connection. Using social media platforms like Facebook and Instagram, he didn't merely showcase images—he told *stories*. These were not rehearsed testimonials or polished soundbites but raw, heartfelt glimpses into people's lives. Some stories were humorous, others heartbreaking, but all were deeply human.

At a time when social media often promotes idealized versions of life, *HONY* cut through the noise by offering something real. People across the world resonated with the vulnerability, honesty, and emotional depth of the stories. Stanton's approach proved that even in the digital space, where screens create physical distance, genuine human connection is possible.

The impact of *HONY* is a powerful reminder that digital communication doesn't have to be cold or detached. People crave realness—stories that evoke empathy and understanding. When we communicate authentically, we bridge gaps, foster connections, and remind each other of our shared humanity.

The digital world is not just about technology—it's about people. Whether you're crafting your digital identity, networking, creating content, or collaborating online, the essence of effective digital communication lies in authenticity. When we embrace empathy, vulnerability, and storytelling, we create meaningful connections that transcend screens. Speaking human in a digital world is not just an art—it's a necessity.

From Digital Native to Digital Pro: Your Career Advantage

Your digital communication skills are a valuable asset in the job market. Here's how to leverage them to your advantage:

- **Highlight Your Skills:** Emphasize your digital communication skills in your resume and cover letter. Provide specific examples of how you've used these skills to achieve positive outcomes.

- **Network Strategically:** Use LinkedIn and other social media platforms to connect with professionals in your field. Attend online networking events and engage in relevant discussions.

- **Showcase Your Portfolio:** Create an online portfolio to showcase your work and demonstrate your skills. This could include writing samples, design projects, or video presentations.

- **Be Adaptable and Lifelong Learners:** The digital landscape is constantly evolving. Be prepared to learn new skills and adapt to new technologies.

The Gen Z Advantage: Embracing the Future of Communication

Gen Z has a unique advantage in the world of communication. You're digital natives, comfortable with technology, and passionate about making a difference. By mastering the principles of digital body language, meaningful conversation, impactful public speaking, and collaborative group culture, you can unlock your full potential and thrive in the 21st-century workplace. "People will forget what you said, people will forget what you did, but people will never forget how you made them feel." - Maya Angelou. This isn't just about getting a job; it's about building a career, making connections, and shaping the future. So, embrace your communication superpower and go out there and conquer the world!

Actionable Exercises:

1. **Empathic Email Revision:** Begin by selecting a recent email or message you believe could have been more considerate. Your task is to rewrite it with a focus on empathy, specifically addressing the recipient's likely emotional state or needs. Incorporate warmer, more approachable language and, where appropriate, add a personal touch to demonstrate understanding. Once both versions are complete, seek feedback from a trusted colleague, asking them to compare the two and identify which resonates more effectively. This process will help you refine your ability to convey empathy in written digital communication.

2. **Tone Experimentation with Feedback Integration:** Craft a single, short message, such as a request or thank you, and compose it in three distinct tones: formal, friendly, and direct. Send each version to a different individual and request specific feedback on how the tone made them feel. Analyze the responses to understand how subtle linguistic choices influence perception. This exercise will provide valuable insights into the impact of tone and help you develop a more nuanced understanding of how to tailor your communication style.

3. **Targeted Empathy Mapping for Specific Scenarios:** Select a digital communication scenario you frequently encounter, such as interacting with a remote team, engaging with customers, or networking on LinkedIn. Develop an empathy map centered on this specific scenario. Identify the feelings, goals, pain points, and communication preferences of the individuals involved. Utilize this map to strategically plan and refine your communication approach in future instances of the same scenario, ensuring it is tailored to meet the needs and expectations of your audience.

4. **Conscious Digital Active Listening:** In an upcoming online discussion, such as a group chat, forum, or comment section, consciously practice active listening. Carefully read each participant's messages, ask clarifying questions without disrupting the conversation's flow, and summarize or acknowledge their points before contributing your own thoughts. Reflect on how this practice affects the overall quality of the conversation and your comprehension of others' viewpoints. This exercise will strengthen your ability to engage meaningfully in digital dialogues.

5. **Humanizing Professional Online Presence:** Review your LinkedIn profile or another professional online profile with a critical eye. Identify areas where you can inject a more human element, such as in your summary, by sharing a personal anecdote, or by showcasing your personality. Implement specific changes to humanize your profile and then solicit feedback from a trusted contact on whether these alterations make you appear more approachable or relatable. This exercise will help you cultivate a more authentic and engaging digital persona.

Key Takeaways:

1. **Digital Empathy is Paramount:** In the absence of face-to-face cues, empathy is crucial for understanding and responding to others' emotions in digital communication.

2. **Context is King:** Always consider the recipient's context (e.g., their workload, mood, culture) before sending a message to tailor your communication for maximum impact.

3. **Human Connection Matters:** Even with digital tools, prioritize human connection by acknowledging emotions, showing empathy, and using a friendly tone.

4. **Nuances of Digital Expression:** Be mindful of the potential for misinterpretation with emojis, GIFs, slang, and tone in text. Prioritize clarity and avoid ambiguity.

5. **Active Listening is Essential:** Practice active listening in digital spaces by carefully reading messages, asking clarifying questions, and acknowledging others' perspectives.

6. **Clarity and Conciseness are Key:** Communicate clearly and concisely, especially in written communication, using bullet points, headings, and short paragraphs.

7. **Choose the Right Channel:** Select the appropriate communication channel (e.g., email, video conferencing, instant messaging) based on the purpose and complexity of the message.

8. **Avoid Common Pitfalls:** Be aware of potential pitfalls such as tone misinterpretation, over-communication, under-communication, timing issues, and assumptions.

9. **Authenticity Builds Connection:** In a digital world that can feel impersonal, authenticity, vulnerability, and storytelling are essential for building genuine human connections.

10. **Digital Communication Skills are a Career Asset:** Develop your digital communication skills to enhance your professional opportunities and thrive in the 21st-century workplace.

Chapter 2

Personal Branding for Gen Z: Building Authority in the Age of Social Media

---

Forget the old-school resumes and stuffy networking events. In today's hyper-connected world, your personal brand is your ultimate career booster. For Gen Z, who practically invented the internet, this isn't just about posting selfies – it's about strategically crafting an online presence that screams YOU and attracts opportunities you never even dreamed of.

Think of it as your digital DNA, a unique blend of skills, passions, and experiences that sets you apart from the crowd. It's about owning your narrative, showcasing your brilliance, and building a community that supports your journey. And in a world where constant evolution is the norm, Robert Greene's insight rings especially true: "The future belongs to those who learn more skills and combine them in creative ways." Your personal brand becomes the canvas upon which you creatively display this unique combination of skills. This isn't about faking it till you make it. It's about being authentically YOU, amplified. Ready to level up your life and build a brand that commands attention? Remember Your Personal Brand is Your Secret Weapon. Let's dive in.

Decoding Your DNA: The Foundation of Your Killer Brand

Before you even think about hitting "post," you need to do some serious soul-searching. This isn't about pretending to be someone you're not; it's about uncovering what makes you.

- **Passion Project Power:** What makes your heart race? What could you talk about for hours on end? Tap into those passions, because that's what will fuel your brand and make you magnetic.

- **Skill Set Supercharge:** Gen Z is the generation of multi-hyphenates. You're not just a student, you're a coder, a photographer, a volunteer, and an Instagram star. Identify your unique skills – both the hard skills you've learned and the soft skills you've mastered through life.

- **Value Alignment Vibe:** What do you stand for? What are your non-negotiables? Your values are your compass, guiding your decisions and attracting the right opportunities. In a world of noise, authenticity shines.

- **Experience Expedition:** Every experience, big or small, has shaped who you are. From that summer internship to leading your college club, own your journey and showcase how it's contributed to your growth.

Crafting Your Digital Persona: The Art of Storytelling

Now that you know what makes you tick, it's time to craft your digital persona. This isn't about creating a fake version of yourself; it's about strategically showcasing your authentic self in a way that resonates with your audience.

- **Narrative Ninja:** Everyone has a story. What's yours? Craft a compelling narrative that highlights your journey, your achievements, and your dreams. Think of it as your personal brand elevator pitch – short, engaging, and unforgettable.

- **Message Maestro:** What's the core message you want to send? What problems can you solve? What makes you different? Keep it clear, concise, and consistent across all platforms.

- **Visual Storyteller:** In the age of Instagram, YouTube, WhatsApp, and Facebook visuals are king. Use high-quality photos and videos to tell your story and showcase your personality. What's your aesthetic? Edgy, classic, quirky? Let your visuals do the talking.

- **Bio Boss:** Your bio is your first impression, so make it count! Keep it short, sweet, and engaging. Highlight your key skills, passions, and experiences, and don't forget a call to action. What do you want people to do after they check out your profile?

Conquering the Digital Landscape: Building Your Tribe

Your online presence is your digital home base. It's where you connect, build your network, and showcase your work. Time to conquer the digital world and build your tribe!

- **Platform Pro:** You don't need to be everywhere. Focus on the platforms that matter most to your industry and your audience. LinkedIn for business, Instagram for creatives, Facebook or YouTube for everyone – choose wisely.

- **Content Creator Extraordinaire:** Content is king, queen, and the entire royal court. Create high-quality, engaging content that provides real value to your audience. Share your insights, experiences, and expertise. Don't be afraid to experiment with different formats – blog posts, videos, podcasts, the works!

- **Engagement Enthusiast:** Building a community isn't just about posting; it's about engaging. Respond to comments, answer questions, and participate in conversations. Show your audience you're listening and that you care.

- **Network Navigator:** Networking is your secret weapon. Connect with people in your industry, both online and offline. Attend events, join online communities, and reach out to people you admire. Remember, it's about building genuine relationships, not just collecting contacts.

Showcasing Your Brilliance: The Art of Self-Promotion (Without Being Annoying)

Self-promotion can feel awkward, but it's crucial for building your brand. The key is to do it strategically and authentically, without coming across as arrogant or self-absorbed.

- **Portfolio Powerhouse:** Your portfolio is your greatest asset. It's a collection of your best work, showcasing your skills and experience. Keep it updated, visually appealing, and easy to navigate.

- **Storytelling Superstar:** Don't just show your work, tell the story behind it. What inspired you? What challenges did you overcome? What did you learn? People connect with stories, not just finished products.

- **Value-Driven Visionary:** Focus on the value you bring. What problems can you solve? How can you make a difference? Highlighting your value proposition will make you irresistible to potential employers and clients.

- **Humility Hacker:** Bragging is a major turn-off. Instead of boasting, focus on sharing your journey and the lessons you've learned. Authenticity and humility are your superpowers.

Staying Ahead of the Curve: The Evolution of Your Brand

The digital world is constantly changing, so your personal brand needs to evolve with it. Staying ahead of the curve requires continuous growth, adaptability, and authenticity.

- **Lifelong Learner:** Never stop learning! Stay updated with industry trends, acquire new skills, and seek out new experiences. The more you learn, the more valuable you become.

- **Adaptability Ace:** Be flexible and adaptable. The ability to pivot and adjust to change is crucial in today's fast-paced world.

- **Feedback Fanatic:** Seek out feedback from your audience, mentors, and peers. Use it to improve your brand and your work.

- **Authenticity Advocate:** Above all, stay true to yourself. Authenticity is your superpower. Don't try to be someone you're not. Let your true personality shine through, and you'll attract the right opportunities and connect with the right people.

The Rise of Oprah Winfrey: The Power of Authenticity

Oprah Winfrey's personal brand is a masterclass in authenticity and emotional connection. Her journey—from growing up in poverty in rural Mississippi to becoming one of the most influential media personalities in the world—was not just about talent or opportunity. It was about her unwavering commitment to being real, vulnerable, and deeply human.

What set Oprah apart was her ability to connect with people on an emotional level. She didn't just interview guests; she created a space where they felt safe to share their stories. Whether discussing personal struggles, societal issues, or self-improvement, she approached every conversation with empathy and sincerity.

Her willingness to share her own challenges—from weight struggles to relationship hurdles and moments of self-doubt—made her more than just a talk show host. She became a symbol of empowerment, transformation, and authenticity. Her brand expanded far beyond television, influencing books, health, spirituality, and philanthropy, yet her core values remained unchanged: inspiring people to live their best lives.

By consistently staying true to herself and her mission, Oprah built a global brand rooted in trust, wisdom, and inspiration—proving that authenticity is the key to lasting influence.

A powerful personal brand is built on authenticity and emotional connection. When people feel they know, trust, and relate to you, it creates a foundation for long-term success. Be real, be adaptable, and keep evolving—because the most influential brands are the ones that stay true to who they are.

The Gen Z Advantage: You Were Born for This

Gen Z, you're digital natives. You've grown up immersed in technology, social media, and a rapidly changing world. This gives you a distinct advantage when it comes to personal branding. You understand the power of online presence, the nuances of digital communication, and the importance of authenticity in a virtual world.

Building Your Tribe: Community is Key

Gen Z understands the power of community. You've grown up connecting with people from all over the world through online platforms. This ability to build and nurture online communities is a valuable asset in the professional world. Your personal brand isn't just about self-promotion; it's about building relationships, connecting with like-minded individuals, and creating a tribe of people who support you and inspire you.

Content is King (and Queen): Share Your Expertise

In the digital age, content is king (and queen). Creating valuable content is one of the most effective ways to build your personal brand and establish yourself as a thought leader. Think about your target audience and what kind of information would be valuable to them. Don't be afraid to experiment with different formats – blog posts, videos, podcasts, infographics – and find what works best for you and your audience.

The Power of "Stupid" Ideas: Embracing Innovation

Gen Z is the generation of innovation. You're not afraid to challenge conventional wisdom and think outside the box. You're comfortable with ambiguity and adaptable to change. These qualities are essential for driving innovation in today's rapidly changing world. Don't be afraid to pursue "stupid" ideas, embrace experimentation, and collaborate with others.

Navigating the Digital Maze: Social Media and Beyond

Social media is an integral part of Gen Z's life. But social media can also be a powerful tool for personal branding and professional growth. Use social media strategically, be authentic, provide value, be consistent, and remember that your online presence is an extension of your personal brand.

Bridging the Gap: From Campus to Career

The transition from college to career can be daunting. But Gen Z has a unique set of skills and experiences that make you well-equipped to navigate this transition. Be proactive, adaptable, resilient, and, most importantly, be yourself.

Mastering the Art of Business: Gen Z Style

Gen Z is redefining entrepreneurship. You're not just following traditional career paths—you're creating your own opportunities, challenging the status quo, and leveraging technology to make an impact. Your generation is tech-savvy, resourceful, and driven by purpose—all essential qualities for success in the modern business world.

Even if you don't plan to start your own company, understanding the fundamentals of business is crucial. Learning by doing, embracing failure as a stepping stone, and taking calculated risks are all part of the journey to mastering the business world—Gen Z style.

Elon Musk: Reinventing the Tech Mogul Persona

Elon Musk is one of the most influential—and controversial—entrepreneurs of our time. His personal brand is a unique blend of innovation, audacity, and disruption, setting him apart from traditional corporate leaders. While many business figures maintain polished, calculated public images, Musk thrives on bold risk-taking and unfiltered engagement, often blurring the line between entrepreneur and entertainer.

What makes Musk's personal brand so powerful?

- **Visionary Leadership:** From Tesla's electric cars to SpaceX's mission to colonize Mars, Musk's ventures are built around revolutionary ideas that push the boundaries of technology and human ambition. His brand is inseparable from his companies—people don't just invest in Tesla or SpaceX; they invest in Musk's vision of the future.

- **Calculated Risk-Taking:** Musk doesn't shy away from failure. He has publicly faced production delays, financial struggles, and engineering setbacks—but rather than hiding from these challenges, he embraces them as part of innovation. His willingness to take massive risks and learn from failure only strengthens his reputation as a trailblazer.

- **Unfiltered Communication:** Unlike traditional CEOs who rely on PR teams to craft their messaging, Musk engages directly with his audience—often through X (Twitter). Whether he's announcing major company updates, debating critics, or sharing memes, his raw and unfiltered communication style makes him feel accessible, unpredictable, and always ahead of the curve.

While Musk's unconventional approach sometimes sparks controversy, it also fuels his magnetic personal brand. He doesn't just sell products; he sells a vision of the future—and millions of people are captivated by it.

A powerful personal brand is built on bold vision, authenticity, and risk-taking. Elon Musk proves that being a disruptor—even when it invites criticism—can create an unstoppable brand. Whether you're building a business or carving out your own career path, aligning your actions with a compelling vision and staying fearlessly authentic is what sets true leaders apart.

The Social Media Trap

Let's talk social media—it's our playground, right? Connecting, networking, building our brands...it's all happening online. But just like anything, there's a flip side.

Think about scrolling; seeing everyone's "highlight reel" can trigger some serious FOMO (Fear of missing out) and make us question our own journey. Remember, curated content isn't the whole story. Let's focus on our own wins and avoid the comparison trap.

Time management is key. Doomscrolling can suck up hours we could be using to level up our skills, connect IRL, or just chill. Finding that balance between online and offline is crucial for success and well-being.

Safety first. The internet's a huge space, and we need to protect our personal info. Think before you share—that data is valuable. Keep your digital footprint clean and professional.

Finally, let's keep it positive. We've all seen the negativity online. Let's use our voices to uplift and support each other. Constructive feedback and positive engagement are way more powerful than online drama.

Social media offers incredible opportunities, but let's navigate it smartly. Authenticity, balance, security, and kindness—these are our superpowers in the digital world. Let's own it.

Build your brand

Building a personal brand is like crafting a unique identity for yourself in the professional world. Here's a breakdown of the key steps involved:

1. **Self-Discovery and Messaging:** Begin by deeply understanding yourself. Identify your strengths, passions, and the values that drive you. What makes you unique? This self-reflection forms the foundation for defining your niche and crafting a compelling brand message. What specific area of expertise do you want to be known for, and what key messages do you want to communicate about your value? Develop a concise and compelling elevator pitch that summarizes who you are and what you do.

2. **Target Audience and Online Presence:** Consider who you are trying to reach. Who are your ideal clients, employers, or collaborators? Understand their needs, interests, and where they spend their time online. This understanding informs where you should focus your efforts. Build a professional online presence, including a website or portfolio showcasing your skills and experience. Optimize your social media profiles with consistent branding and messaging, targeting the platforms where your audience is active.

3. **Content Creation and Engagement:** Share valuable content that demonstrates your expertise and provides value to your target audience. This could include blog posts, articles, videos, or social media updates. Content creation establishes you as a thought leader and attracts your ideal audience. Actively engage with your audience online. Respond to comments, participate in discussions, and build relationships with your followers.

4. **Networking and Relationship Building:** Connect with other professionals in your field. Attend industry events and conferences, engage in online communities, and build relationships with influencers in your niche. Networking expands your reach, opens doors to new opportunities, and provides valuable insights.

5. **Consistency and Authenticity:** Maintain a consistent brand identity across all platforms, using the same visuals, messaging, and tone of voice. Be authentic and genuine. Let your personality shine through and be true to yourself. Consistency and authenticity build trust and credibility with your audience.

6. **Monitoring, Evaluation, and Adaptation:** Track your progress by monitoring your website traffic, social media engagement, and other relevant metrics. Gather feedback from your network and audience to understand how your brand is perceived. Be flexible and willing to adapt your strategy based on what works best. Regularly evaluate your efforts and make adjustments to ensure you are effectively building your personal brand.

Building a personal brand takes time and effort, but it's a valuable investment in your career. By focusing on these six key steps, you can create a strong and authentic brand that helps you stand out and achieve your professional goals.

Your Brand, Your Legacy

Personal branding is more than just a buzzword; it's a skill that can define your career trajectory in the age of social media. By blending authenticity with strategy, leveraging the right platforms, and consistently sharing your expertise, you can build a brand that not only opens doors but also reflects who you truly are. Personal branding is a journey, and every post, connection, and interaction is a step toward building your unique legacy.

Actionable Exercises:

1. **Define Your Unique Value Proposition:** Start by writing down three things that make you stand out in your field. Use these points to create a short statement that says what you do and who you help. This statement should be something

you can easily put in your social media bios. For example, "I help young entrepreneurs launch their startups by providing digital marketing strategies."

2. **Develop Content Pillars:** Figure out 3-5 main topics you want to be known for online. These topics will guide what you post and make sure you consistently show your expertise. For example, if you're a graphic designer, your pillars might be "design tips," "portfolio showcases," and "industry trends."

3. **Conduct a Social Media Audit:** Go through all your social media profiles and check if they match the image you want to project. Make sure your profile pictures, bios, and any pinned posts reflect your skills and personality. Update anything that doesn't fit your personal brand.

4. **Create a 30-Day Content Plan:** Challenge yourself to post something relevant to your personal brand every day for 30 days. Mix up your content with educational posts, inspirational messages, and personal stories. This will help you stay consistent and show your expertise to your audience.

5. **Create and Share Your Elevator Pitch:** Make a short video or write a post where you introduce yourself and explain what you do. Use your unique value proposition to clearly state your skills and invite people to connect with you. This is a fantastic way to start networking and building your online presence.

Key Takeaways:

1. **Authenticity is Key:** Your personal brand should reflect your true self, not a fabricated persona.

2. **Define Your Niche:** Clearly identify your area of expertise and what makes you unique.

3. **Craft a Compelling Narrative:** Tell your story in a way that engages and resonates with your audience.

4. **Consistency Matters:** Maintain a consistent brand message and visual identity across all platforms.

5. **Provide Value:** Share content that educates, informs, or entertains your audience.

6. **Engage Actively:** Don't just post; interact with your audience through comments and conversations.

7. **Network Strategically:** Build genuine relationships with people in your industry.

8. **Showcase Your Work:** Create a portfolio that highlights your skills and achievements.

9. **Adapt and Evolve:** Be prepared to adjust your brand as you grow and the digital landscape changes.

10. **Use Social Media Wisely:** Leverage platforms strategically to build your brand and connect with your audience.

Chapter 3

STORYTELLING FOR IMPACT: THE ART OF PERSUASION AND INFLUENCE

"The most powerful person in the world is the storyteller. The storyteller sets the vision, values, and agenda of an entire generation that is to come." – Steve Jobs

In today's information-saturated world, storytelling isn't just a nice-to-have; it's a *must-have* superpower. It's the key that unlocks connection, persuasion, and influence, setting apart exceptional leaders, negotiators, and professionals. For Gen Z, a generation fluent in digital communication, mastering storytelling is more crucial than ever. It's the ability to cut through the noise, captivate your audience, and leave a lasting impression.

This chapter is your guide to harnessing the power of narrative. We'll explore how to craft stories that resonate, evoke emotion, and drive meaningful change. Get ready to unleash your inner storyteller and make your voice impossible to ignore.

The Power of Narrative: Why Stories Matter

Since the dawn of time, stories have been our way of making sense of the world. They're how we pass down knowledge, share experiences, and inspire action. In a world drowning in data, stories are the life raft of meaning. They connect with us on a deeply human level, bypassing logic and going straight to the heart.

For Gen Z, a generation that values authenticity and connection, storytelling is the perfect vehicle for expressing who you are, what you believe in, and the unique value you bring.

Crafting Your Career Narrative: Making Yourself Unforgettable

Your career narrative isn't a dry list of job titles; it's the story of your professional journey. It's how you showcase your skills, values, and growth. A well-crafted narrative makes you memorable, setting you apart from the crowd.

Instead of simply stating, "I have experience in project management," tell a story: "When our team was facing a critical deadline, I stepped up to streamline our workflow. By implementing agile methodologies and fostering open communication, we not only met the deadline but also delivered the project under budget. This experience taught me the power of proactive problem-solving and collaborative leadership."

This approach reveals your skills, your thought process, and your impact. It's not just about what you did; it's about *how* you did it and what you learned along the way.

Data with Heart: Weaving Facts into Compelling Narratives

Data is powerful, but it's even more powerful when woven into a compelling story. Instead of presenting dry statistics, connect the numbers to human experiences and relatable outcomes.

Imagine you're presenting to your team about improving customer satisfaction. Instead of just showing a chart, tell a story: "Last quarter, we saw a dip in customer satisfaction scores. By analyzing customer feedback and implementing targeted training programs for our support team, we were able to improve our scores by 15%, resulting in increased customer loyalty and positive reviews. This shows how investing in our team directly impacts our customers and our bottom line."

This narrative connects the data to real-world impact, making it more meaningful and memorable.

Creating a compelling data story involves several key steps. First, define your purpose and audience, tailoring your message and delivery to their understanding and desired outcome. Next, gather and analyze relevant, credible data, identifying patterns and insights that support your narrative. Craft this narrative with a clear beginning, middle, and end, incorporating storytelling elements to engage your audience. Visually represent your data with simple, clear charts and graphs that effectively communicate your key findings. Choose the appropriate medium for sharing your story, whether it's a presentation, report, or interactive dashboard, and practice your delivery for a smooth and confident presentation. Remember to keep your story concise, using plain language and, where appropriate, personal anecdotes to connect with your audience and ensure your message is both informative and engaging.

The 3 Cs of Storytelling: Clarity, Connection, Confidence

Effective storytelling rests on three pillars:

- **Clarity:** Keep your message concise and focused. Avoid jargon and unnecessary details. Brevity is key to capturing and holding attention.

- **Connection:** Tap into universal emotions and experiences. Know your audience and tailor your story to their values and aspirations.

- **Confidence:** Practice your delivery. Maintain eye contact, vary your tone, and use pauses for emphasis. Your passion for the story will be contagious.

The SUCCESs Model: Crafting Sticky Ideas

Want your ideas to stick? The SUCCESs model provides a powerful framework:

- **Simple:** Boil down your message to its core essence.

- **Unexpected:** Surprise your audience and break the pattern.

- **Concrete:** Use vivid imagery and real-life examples.

- **Credible:** Back up your claims with evidence and testimonials.

- **Emotional:** Tap into emotions to make your message resonate.

- **Stories:** Weave your ideas into compelling narratives.

The Power of a Sticky Idea: The Blue Dot Campaign

Simple:

In 1990, astronomer Carl Sagan convinced NASA to turn the Voyager 1 spacecraft around for one last photo of Earth. The image captured our planet as a tiny blue dot floating in the vast emptiness of space.

Unexpected:

At the time, space photos typically showcased planets in stunning detail. But this? A barely visible speck in an infinite cosmos. It was almost too small to matter—yet it changed everything.

Concrete:

Sagan used this image to explain how fragile and interconnected humanity truly is. He described Earth as a "pale blue dot," emphasizing that every war, every love story, every person who ever lived existed on this tiny speck, suspended in a sunbeam.

Credible:

Sagan, a world-renowned scientist, wasn't just offering poetic musings—he was presenting a perspective grounded in astrophysics, planetary science, and the reality of our place in the universe.

Emotional:

The image stirred something deep within people. It humbled us. It made us reflect on our divisions, our conflicts, and our shared responsibility to protect our home.

Stories:

Sagan's message didn't end with facts; it became a story of unity and perspective—one that has influenced environmental movements, global cooperation, and even how we think about life beyond Earth.

A simple, unexpected image—just a tiny dot—became one of the most powerful narratives about our existence. That's the power of a sticky idea.

Building a Brand Narrative: Your Story, Your Impact

Your brand narrative is the story you tell about yourself or your organization. It's how you communicate your values, your mission, and your unique value proposition. Use the seven-part story framework to craft a compelling brand narrative:

1. **Character (Your Customer):** Focus on your audience's needs and desires.

2. **Problem:** Clearly define the challenge your audience faces.

3. **Guide (Your Brand):** Position your brand as the solution.

4. **Plan:** Offer a clear path for your audience to follow.

5. **Call to Action:** Encourage immediate engagement.

6. **Stakes:** Highlight what's at risk if they don't act.

7. **Success:** Paint a picture of the positive outcome.

A Sustainable Fashion Brand - "EcoWear"

1. **Character:**

   Meet Sarah, a young professional who loves fashion but is increasingly concerned about the environmental impact of fast fashion. She wants stylish yet sustainable clothing that aligns with her values.

2. **Problem:**

   Sarah struggles to find affordable, high-quality, eco-friendly outfits. Many brands claim to be sustainable but lack transparency about their materials and ethical practices.

3. **Guide:**

   Enter EcoWear, a brand committed to sustainability, ethical production, and timeless fashion. EcoWear uses organic fabrics, fair-trade labour, and transparent supply chains to create stylish outfits with a conscience.

4. **Plan:**

   EcoWear provides a simple way for Sarah to make sustainable choices. The website offers clear information on materials, production processes, and impact. Plus, they have a "Wear & Care" guide to help customers extend the life of their clothing.

5. **Call to Action:**

   "Join the sustainable fashion movement today! Browse our latest collection and make a difference with every purchase."

6. **Stakes:**

   If Sarah continues supporting fast fashion, she contributes to waste, pollution, and unfair labour practices. By choosing EcoWear, she helps protect the environment and supports ethical fashion.

7. **Success:**

Sarah feels empowered knowing her fashion choices align with her values. She receives compliments on her stylish outfits and proudly shares EcoWear's mission with friends, inspiring them to shop sustainably too.

This framework ensures your brand story connects emotionally with your audience, making them feel understood, engaged, and motivated to take action.

Transforming Presentations: From Dull to Dynamic

Transform your presentations from snooze-fests to captivating experiences by incorporating storytelling:

- Start with a Hook: Grab attention with a surprising statistic, a provocative question, or a compelling anecdote.

- Structure with a Narrative Arc: Set up the problem, introduce the solution, and conclude with a powerful call to action.

- Use Visual Storytelling: Enhance your message with impactful visuals.

Apple's "Think Different" Campaign – The Power of Identity in Persuasion

In 1997, Apple launched its groundbreaking "Think Different" campaign—not just as an ad but as a movement. It wasn't about selling computers. It was about selling a mindset, a philosophy, and an identity.

At a time when Apple was struggling, this campaign redefined its narrative. Instead of highlighting technical specifications or product features, Apple told a story that resonated with its audience's sense of self. The campaign featured visionary figures like Albert Einstein, Mahatma Gandhi, and Martin Luther King Jr.—people who dared to challenge norms and change the world.

The message was clear: Apple wasn't just a tech company; it was a brand for those who saw themselves as rebels, visionaries, and innovators.

By aligning Apple with creativity, disruption, and change, the campaign spoke directly to its audience's aspirations. It persuaded not through logic but through identity and emotion. People didn't just buy Apple products; they became part of a movement that stood for thinking differently.

The result? A brand transformation that reignited Apple's influence and set the stage for its future success.

The most persuasive stories are those that connect with people's identities. When your message aligns with who your audience is—or who they aspire to be—it doesn't just inform or convince. It inspires action and builds loyalty that lasts.

Storytelling in Job Interviews and Negotiations: Show, Don't Just Tell

Facts tell; stories sell. Facts and figures matter, but stories make you memorable. Whether you're in a job interview or negotiating a salary, storytelling helps you showcase your skills, experience, and impact in a way that connects emotionally and demonstrates real value.

Why Storytelling Works

People don't just remember facts—they remember narratives. A well-told story: Engages the interviewer and makes your experience stand out. Demonstrates problem-solving, leadership, and adaptability in real-world scenarios. Builds credibility and trust, making it easier to justify your worth in negotiations.

How to Use Storytelling in Interviews

Instead of saying, *"I have strong leadership skills,"*

Tell a story:

"In my previous role, our team faced a major product launch delay due to supply chain issues. I initiated a cross-functional task force, restructured timelines, and collaborated with key suppliers. As a result, we reduced delays by 40% and successfully launched ahead of competitors."

Use the **STAR method** to structure your stories:

♦　**Situation:** Set the stage with context.

♦　**Task:** Define the challenge or goal.

♦　**Action:** Explain what you did to address the situation.

♦　**Result:** Share the impact or outcome.

Using Storytelling in Negotiations

Rather than stating, *"I deserve a higher salary,"*

Frame it with a story:

"Over the past year, I led a project that streamlined our client onboarding, reducing turnaround time by 30% and increasing customer satisfaction scores to a record high. The efficiencies I implemented saved the company over $500K annually. Given this impact, I believe a salary adjustment to reflect my contributions is justified."

Numbers impress, but stories persuade. Whether landing a job or negotiating better terms, stories make your case compelling, relatable, and hard to ignore.

Storytelling for Different Platforms: Tailoring Your Approach

Each platform has unique strengths—adapt your storytelling to maximize impact:

♦　**YouTube:** Engaging videos with trending audio, optimized for retention.

- **Instagram:** Visually compelling content paired with concise, scroll-stopping captions.

- **LinkedIn:** Thought-provoking insights, professional storytelling, and industry leadership.

- **X (formerly Twitter):** Sharp, impactful messages that drive real-time conversations.

The Power of Vulnerability: Building Authentic Connections

Authenticity is key, especially for Gen Z. Don't be afraid to show your vulnerability. Share your struggles, your failures, and the lessons you've learned. Vulnerability builds trust and creates genuine connection.

Mastering Story Structure: The ABT Framework

The ABT (And, But, Therefore) framework offers a simple yet powerful structure for crafting compelling narratives:

- **And:** Establish the context.

- **But:** Introduce the conflict.

- **Therefore:** Provide the resolution and takeaway.

The Unexpected Promotion: An ABT Story

And: Lisa had been excelling in her role as a marketing analyst, consistently delivering high-quality work and building strong relationships with clients. She loved her job and was eager to grow within the company.

But: Despite her dedication, she kept getting passed over for promotions. Her manager praised her work but told her she needed to "be more visible." Frustrated, she realized that just working hard wasn't enough—she had to advocate for herself.

Therefore: Lisa started sharing her successes in team meetings, volunteered to lead a high-impact project, and built relationships with senior leaders. Within six months, her efforts paid off—she not only got promoted but also became a mentor, helping others take charge of their careers.

Hard work matters, but visibility and strategic self-advocacy can be the game-changers that open doors.

The Power of Visionary Storytelling: Inspiring Change Through Narrative

Great leaders, speakers, and change-makers don't just present facts—they tell stories that inspire action. Whether in business, leadership, or social movements, visionary storytelling has the power to unite people under a shared purpose and drive meaningful change.

One of the most profound examples of this is Dr. Martin Luther King Jr.'s "I Have a Dream" speech, a masterclass in storytelling that shaped history. Through vivid imagery, emotional depth, and a compelling vision of the future, Dr. King moved millions and fuelled the Civil Rights Movement.

Let's explore how storytelling with vision can transform ideas into movements and inspire action.

In 1963, Dr. Martin Luther King Jr. delivered one of the most powerful and influential speeches in American history—his "I Have a Dream" speech. It wasn't just his words that resonated with millions of people, but the way he told a story. Dr. King used storytelling as a tool to inspire action, convey hope, and call for social change during the Civil Rights Movement.

What made this speech particularly impactful was Dr. King's ability to paint a vivid picture of a better future. Instead of focusing solely on the injustice and inequality of the time, he shared a compelling vision of what America could become—an America where people of all races would live in harmony. His story was one of hope, transformation, and the pursuit of a shared dream, which connected deeply with his audience's emotions and aspirations.

Dr. King's speech is a brilliant example of how storytelling can create a sense of unity and purpose. By using metaphors, such as "the red hills of Georgia" and "the heat of oppression," he helped listeners visualize a future they longed for. He didn't just talk about racial equality; he made it feel real. He painted a mental picture of a world where all children—regardless of color—could play together in peace. This storytelling technique went beyond simply persuading; it moved hearts and minds, motivating people to take action for social justice.

The art of persuasion and influence in this speech didn't lie solely in the facts or logical arguments—it was in the story he told. Dr. King understood that people are not just persuaded by statistics or data, but by stories that tap into their emotions, desires, and visions for a better world.

Storytelling for impact involves crafting a compelling vision that taps into emotions and inspires action. When you share a story that paints a vivid, aspirational picture, you can persuade and influence people to act on that vision.

Storytelling as a Superpower: Unleash Your Potential

"The most powerful way to change the world is to tell a good story." - Robert McKee. This isn't just a clever saying; it's a fundamental truth. Storytelling is more than just a skill; it's a superpower because it allows us to bridge gaps, evoke emotions, and inspire action. By crafting narratives that resonate, we don't just share information; we create shared experiences and spark genuine connection. It's how you connect, influence, and make a difference. By mastering the art of storytelling, you can unlock your full potential and shape not only your future, but the future of those you touch with your stories.

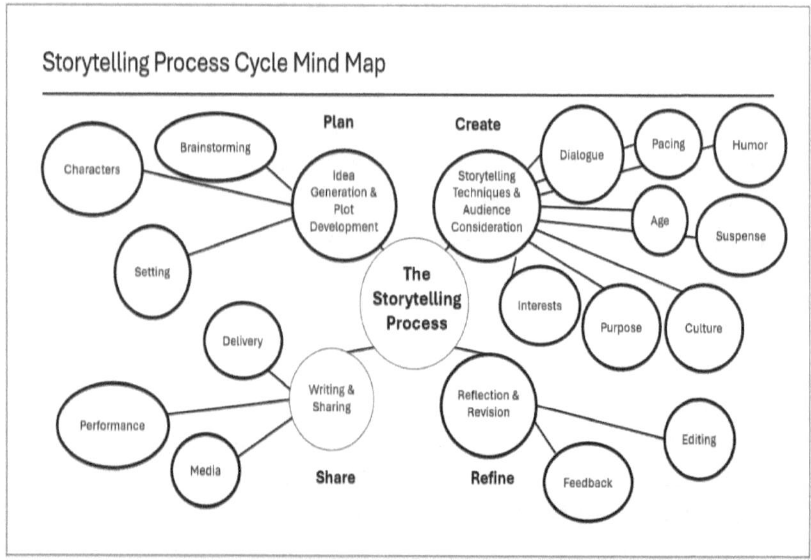

Actionable Exercises:

1. **Craft Your Origin Story:** Take a moment to write a short paragraph about how you or your brand started. Include who you are, what challenge you faced, how you overcame it, and what lesson or value you now share with others. After writing it, share it with someone and ask for their feedback to make it even better.

2. **Practice the 3-Act Structure:** Pick a recent experience from your life, either personal or professional, and structure it like a story with three parts: the setup, the conflict, and the resolution. First, introduce the context and characters. Then, describe the challenge or turning point. Finally, share the outcome and what you learned. Use this structure to create a compelling story you can share in a meeting or on social media.

3. **Story Sparking Exercise:** Write down three events from your life or career that taught you something valuable. For each

event, note the situation, the conflict, the resolution, and the lesson you learned. Then, choose one of these events and refine it into a story you can use to inspire or persuade others.

4. **Analyze a Great Story:** Choose a TED Talk, movie, or book that you find really engaging. Watch or read it and pay attention to how the storyteller grabs your attention, how the story makes you feel, and what techniques they use, like pacing or imagery. Then, try to use one of those techniques in your next story.

5. **Create a Story Bank:** Start a collection of your own stories by writing down impactful moments, challenges, and successes as they happen. Over time, this collection will become a resource you can use to craft persuasive stories.

Key Takeaways:

1. **Stories Connect:** Stories bypass logic and connect with people on an emotional level, making them more memorable than facts alone.

2. **Narrative is Powerful:** Your career narrative or brand story helps you showcase your skills, values, and impact in a compelling way.

3. **Data Needs Heart:** Data is more powerful when woven into a story that connects numbers to human experiences and relatable outcomes.

4. **Clarity, Connection, Confidence:** Effective storytelling relies on keeping your message clear, connecting with your audience, and delivering your story with confidence.

5. **SUCCESs Model:** Use the SUCCESs model (Simple, Unexpected, Concrete, Credible, Emotional, Stories) to make your ideas stick.

6. **Brand Narrative Matters:** Craft a brand narrative that communicates your values, mission, and unique value proposition.

7. **Presentations Can Be Stories:** Transform presentations by using storytelling techniques like starting with a hook and structuring with a narrative arc.

8. **Vulnerability Builds Trust:** Don't be afraid to show vulnerability; it builds trust and creates genuine connections.

9. **ABT Framework:** Use the ABT (And, But, Therefore) framework to structure your stories and make them more compelling.

10. **Visionary Storytelling Inspires:** Use storytelling to inspire change and unite people under a shared purpose.

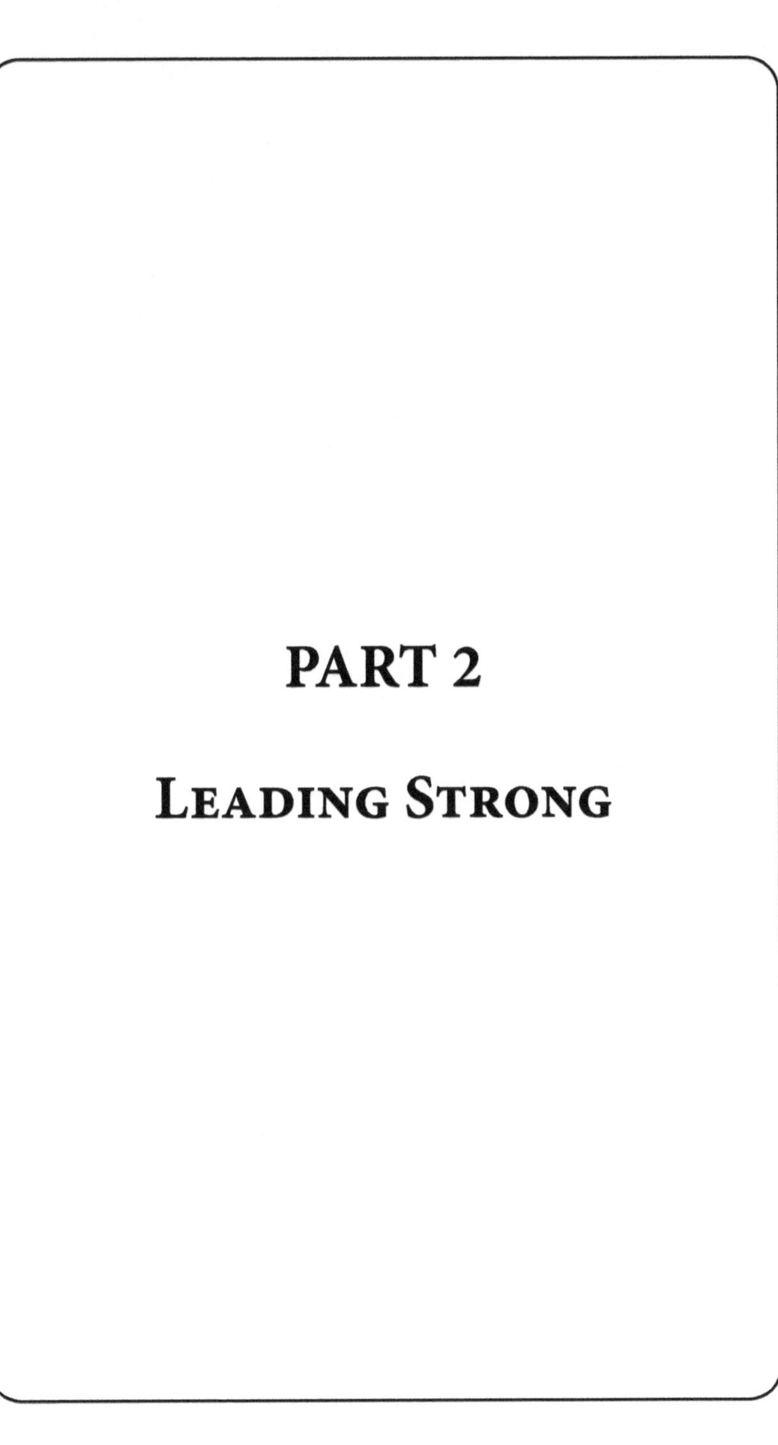

PART 2

LEADING STRONG

Chapter 4

EMOTIONAL INTELLIGENCE 2.0: THRIVING IN DIVERSE AND INCLUSIVE WORKPLACES

In today's dynamic and ever-evolving workplace, people from diverse backgrounds, cultures, and experiences come together to collaborate, create, and innovate. While technical skills remain crucial, they are no longer the sole determinants of professional success. The ability to navigate emotions—both your own and those of others—has become a game-changer. Enter Emotional Intelligence (EQ), the secret sauce that empowers individuals to build meaningful relationships, manage conflicts gracefully, and lead with empathy. This chapter delves into EQ 2.0, a refined and actionable approach to emotional intelligence that helps professionals, particularly Gen Z, excel in diverse and inclusive workplaces. "To handle yourself, use your head; to handle others, use your heart." - Eleanor Roosevelt. This perfectly encapsulates the essence of EQ.

Emotional Intelligence (EI) and Emotional Intelligence 2.0 both emphasize the importance of understanding and managing emotions but take different approaches. Emotional Intelligence explores the depth and accuracy of EI, offering a comprehensive examination of its foundations, including self-awareness, emotional regulation, and understanding others' emotions. While highly informative, it can be dense and challenging to read. In contrast, Emotional Intelligence 2.0 focuses on clarity and practical application, making it more accessible to beginners or those seeking actionable strategies. It emphasizes self-awareness, self-management, social awareness, and relationship management, providing specific tools to enhance emotional intelligence in everyday life. Emotional Intelligence offers a deep dive for those seeking an academic perspective, whereas Emotional Intelligence 2.0 is ideal for readers who prefer practical, easy-to-implement advice.

Figure: Feelings and Emotions – Facial Expressions

EQ 2.0: The Bridge Between Knowledge and Action

Understanding emotions is one thing, but applying emotional intelligence in real-life scenarios is where the magic happens. EQ 2.0 goes beyond traditional theories, equipping individuals with practical strategies to enhance self-awareness, self-management, social awareness, and relationship management. Gen Z, known for their adaptability and desire for real-world impact, can leverage

EQ 2.0 to build thriving careers and cultivate positive workplace environments.

Self-Awareness: The Gateway to Personal and Professional 10x Growth

Picture this: You Walk into a meeting, and something feels off. Maybe you're anxious, irritated, or uncertain. But do you know why? Self-awareness is about tuning into these emotions, recognizing their origins, and understanding how they influence your actions. It's the foundation of emotional intelligence and a critical skill for workplace success.

♦ **The Power of Self-Reflection:** Journaling your thoughts, practicing mindfulness, and seeking constructive feedback can help uncover emotional patterns and triggers.

♦ **Decoding Emotional Triggers:** Identifying the situations that provoke strong emotional reactions enables you to develop strategies to navigate them effectively.

♦ **Understanding Your Core Values:** What truly motivates you? What principles guide your decisions? When you align your actions with your core values, you build authenticity and confidence in your professional journey.

The Courage to Ask

Carlos, a software engineer from São Paulo, joined a new team in Berlin. His technical skills were undeniable, but he quickly realized that navigating the cultural nuances of his new workplace was a different challenge altogether. The German team valued directness, a stark contrast to Carlos's culture, which prioritized politeness and indirect communication.

Initially, Carlos found himself constantly second-guessing his own perceptions. He noticed a recurring flaw in the code review process, but he hesitated to speak up. "Am I being too sensitive?" he wondered. "Perhaps I'm misinterpreting their intentions?" This internal dialogue reflected a lack of self-awareness—Carlos wasn't yet tuned into his own discomfort and how it was impacting his behavior. He was suppressing his genuine observations, fearing he might offend his colleagues.

The delays caused by the flawed process began to pile up, creating a palpable tension within the team. Carlos could feel his anxiety growing, but he still couldn't pinpoint the exact source of his unease. He was experiencing emotions, but he wasn't yet aware of the triggers and how they were influencing his actions.

One day, during a team retrospective, the manager, Lena, noticed Carlos's hesitation. She sensed his internal struggle and decided to intervene. "Carlos," she said, "you bring a fresh perspective. Is there something we could improve?"

This simple question acted as a catalyst. It forced Carlos to confront his internal conflict. He took a deep breath, consciously acknowledging his fear and the importance of his observation. He realized that his hesitation wasn't just about cultural differences; it was also about his own lack of self-awareness. He was finally tuning into his emotions and understanding their origins.

"Yes," Carlos replied, "I've noticed a recurring issue with the code review process." He then shared his observations and proposed an alternative workflow. His suggestion was not only accepted but also praised for its clarity and efficiency.

This moment marked a turning point for Carlos. He had begun to develop a deeper understanding of his own emotional patterns and triggers. He realized that his fear of offending others was preventing him from contributing his best work. By becoming more self-aware, he was able to align his actions with his core value of contributing to the team's success.

Encouraged by the positive reception, Carlos began to participate more actively. He started to recognize the situations that triggered his anxiety and developed strategies to manage them. Months later, when a new hire from India joined the team,

Carlos made it a point to mentor her, ensuring she felt comfortable navigating cultural differences. He used his newfound self-awareness to understand her potential struggles and created a safe space for her to grow.

Emotional intelligence, particularly self-awareness, empowers individuals to recognize their emotional patterns and triggers. By tuning into their emotions, professionals can overcome cultural barriers, align their actions with their core values, and create safe spaces for honest dialogue and collective growth. Carlos's journey shows that by becoming more self-aware, he was able to navigate cultural differences, contributing his best work and becoming a mentor to others.

Self-Management: Mastering the Art of Emotional Agility

Life is unpredictable, and so is the workplace. How you respond to challenges, stress, and setbacks defines your ability to succeed. Self-management is not about suppressing emotions but rather channelling them in ways that serve you and those around you.

- **Emotional Regulation Hacks:** Deep breathing, cognitive reframing, and practicing gratitude can help you stay grounded in high-pressure situations.

- **Building Resilience:** Learning from setbacks, maintaining a positive perspective, and leaning on a strong support system can help you bounce back from adversity with renewed energy.

- **The Adaptability Mindset:** The ability to embrace change and approach new challenges with curiosity and flexibility makes you invaluable in today's fast-moving workplace.

The Silent Apology

In a bustling marketing agency, Mei, a project manager from Shanghai, was leading a high-pressure campaign with a multicultural team. James, a creative director from New York, and

Aisha, a copywriter from Nairobi, were key players. The project demanded rapid brainstorming and collaboration, but cultural differences in communication styles were creating friction.

During a critical meeting, James, known for his assertive style, repeatedly interrupted Aisha while she was sharing her ideas. Mei noticed Aisha's body language change—she leaned back, crossed her arms, and withdrew from the discussion. James, oblivious, continued to dominate.

Mei felt a surge of frustration. She recognized the potential for conflict and the impact it could have on the team's morale and productivity. However, instead of reacting impulsively, she consciously employed self-management techniques. She took a moment to regulate her emotions, reminding herself that her role was to facilitate a productive environment, not to escalate the situation.

After the meeting, Mei invited Aisha for coffee. She listened attentively as Aisha expressed her frustration, validating her feelings without judgment. Mei practiced empathy, understanding that Aisha's reaction stemmed from feeling undervalued. Instead of immediately confronting James, Mei chose to manage her own impulse to intervene directly. She knew that a more nuanced approach was needed.

Mei then engaged in cognitive reframing. She shifted her perspective from viewing the situation as a problem to seeing it as an opportunity to improve team dynamics. She reflected on the team's need for a structured communication process and decided to introduce a "listening stick" in future meetings. This strategy allowed her to channel her frustration into a constructive solution.

The following day, Mei introduced the "listening stick" concept. Explaining that only the person holding it could speak, she ensured everyone had an equal opportunity to contribute. While initially met with skepticism, the practice transformed their discussions into thoughtful, balanced exchanges. Mei remained adaptable, adjusting the process as needed and encouraging the team to provide feedback.

Later, James, after observing the positive impact of the "listening stick," privately apologized to Aisha, admitting he hadn't realized his behavior was discouraging. This demonstrated Mei's effective self-management; her controlled response and proactive solution facilitated a resolution without direct confrontation. The team began to embrace diverse perspectives, leading to a campaign that resonated with global audiences.

Self-management involves regulating emotions, channeling them effectively, and adapting to challenging situations. Mei's story illustrates how emotional agility, cognitive reframing, and proactive problem-solving can transform potential conflicts into opportunities for growth. By managing her own impulses and emotions, she fostered a more inclusive and productive team environment, showcasing the power of self-management in achieving collaborative success.

Social Awareness: Reading Between the Lines in Human Interaction

Have you ever felt a shift in the room without anyone saying a word? Social awareness is about picking up on these subtle cues—understanding the emotions of those around you and responding with empathy and sensitivity.

♦ **Cultivating Empathy:** Active listening, asking insightful questions, and genuinely caring about others' perspectives can help build stronger connections.

♦ **Navigating Cultural Nuances:** The modern workplace is a melting pot of cultures. Being aware of different communication styles and emotional expressions fosters inclusive and effective collaboration.

♦ **Mastering Nonverbal Communication:** A slight change in tone, body language, or facial expressions can convey more than words. Learning to read these cues can significantly improve your interpersonal interactions.

The Unseen Impact of Inclusion

Rajiv, a senior manager at a multinational pharmaceutical firm, considered himself a proponent of inclusivity. However, he soon realized that true inclusivity required more than just good intentions. He faced a significant challenge when integrating Priya, a visually impaired software engineer, into a fast-paced product development project.

During Priya's first presentation, Rajiv's social awareness was heightened. He observed the subtle shifts in his team's demeanor. He noticed the averted glances, the slight hesitations, and the overall disengagement. He recognized the nonverbal cues that spoke volumes: his team was making assumptions based on Priya's disability, subconsciously questioning her potential contributions.

Rajiv also paid close attention to Priya's body language. He saw her determined posture, her slightly strained voice, and the subtle signs of her struggle to connect. He recognized her desire to prove her value, but he also sensed her growing frustration and isolation. Rajiv's ability to read these emotional cues allowed him to understand the underlying tension in the room.

Recognizing the need for a shift in perspective, Rajiv decided to cultivate empathy within his team. He understood that simply telling them to be inclusive wouldn't suffice. He needed to create an experience that would allow them to truly understand Priya's reality.

He arranged an empathy-building workshop where team members experienced simulated disabilities, such as navigating the workplace blindfolded. This immersive experience allowed them to step into Priya's shoes, fostering a deeper understanding of her daily challenges. It was a powerful demonstration of how different lived experiences can shape perceptions and interactions.

The breakthrough came during a brainstorming session for an accessibility feature. Here, Priya's lived experience became invaluable. Rajiv, having heightened his social awareness, recognized the moment of opportunity. He actively listened to Priya, asking insightful questions that encouraged her to share her unique perspective. He understood that her insights were not just about technical solutions; they were about understanding the user experience from a different point of view.

Rajiv amplified Priya's contributions by publicly celebrating her innovative ideas. He consciously shifted the team's mindset from skepticism to respect by highlighting the value of diverse perspectives and experiences. His actions demonstrated a deep understanding of the emotional and social dynamics at play.

Months later, Priya became a mentor for new hires with disabilities, fostering a culture of inclusion that extended beyond her immediate team. Rajiv's social awareness had created a ripple effect, transforming the workplace into a more empathetic and inclusive environment.

Social awareness, particularly empathy, the ability to navigate different lived experiences, and the mastery of nonverbal communication, are essential for fostering inclusive workplaces. Rajiv's story demonstrates how recognizing and responding to emotional cues can transform perceptions and unlock hidden potential. By cultivating empathy and promoting understanding, leaders can create environments where every team member feels valued and empowered.

Relationship Management: The Key to Influence and Collaboration

In a professional world driven by teamwork, influence, and leadership, the ability to cultivate and maintain strong relationships is invaluable. Relationship management encompasses everything from clear communication to conflict resolution and the ability to inspire and motivate others.

- Becoming a Communication Pro: Great communicators don't just talk—they listen, clarify, and adapt their messages to resonate with different audiences.

- Transforming Conflict into Collaboration: Workplace conflicts are inevitable but handling them with emotional intelligence turns challenges into opportunities for growth and deeper understanding.

- The Art of Teamwork: A high-EQ professional knows how to foster trust, encourage diverse perspectives, and unite people toward a common goal.

The Quiet Victory of a Newcomer

Amara, a recent graduate, joined a global tech company eager to contribute. The diverse and inclusive workplace, however, presented a unique challenge: her team was comprised of colleagues from seven different nationalities, each with distinct communication styles and work habits. Amara recognized that building strong relationships would be crucial to her success.

Within her first week, Amara observed a growing tension between two senior teammates, Lisa and Ahmed, concerning a project delay. Lisa, from a culture that values direct communication, expressed her frustrations bluntly. Ahmed, from a culture that prioritized harmony, preferred a more subtle approach. Amara understood that this clash of communication styles was impeding collaboration.

Instead of feeling overwhelmed, Amara decided to actively manage the situation. She focused on building rapport with both Lisa and Ahmed, taking time to understand their individual perspectives and communication preferences. She recognized that effective relationship management required her to adapt her communication style to resonate with each of them.

During a team meeting, Amara demonstrated her ability to transform conflict into collaboration. She recognized that direct confrontation would likely exacerbate the tension. Instead, she asked a neutral, open-ended question:

"What do you both think is the biggest challenge we're facing with this project?"

This simple question served as a catalyst for constructive dialogue. Amara's ability to communicate clearly and empathetically created a safe space for Lisa to express her concerns without feeling attacked and for Ahmed to share his perspective without feeling dismissed. She actively listened, clarifying points and ensuring both parties felt heard and understood.

Amara then facilitated a collaborative brainstorming session, suggesting a "middle ground" approach that incorporated elements of both Lisa's and Ahmed's preferred methods. This demonstrated her ability to foster teamwork by uniting people toward a common goal. She encouraged open communication, ensured everyone had an opportunity to contribute, and facilitated the creation of a shared solution.

By skillfully managing the conflict and fostering collaboration, Amara showcased her exceptional relationship management skills. She earned the trust and respect of her colleagues, establishing herself as a valuable team member. Her ability to read emotions, respect cultural differences, and mediate effectively earned her a reputation as a rising star in the company.

Relationship management involves cultivating strong relationships, transforming conflict into collaboration, and fostering teamwork through effective communication and mediation. Amara's story highlights how a newcomer can leverage these skills to navigate diverse workplaces, build trust, and facilitate positive outcomes. By focusing on empathy, clear communication, and collaborative problem-solving, professionals can foster strong relationships and create a harmonious and productive work environment.

The Gen Z Advantage: Emotional Intelligence as a Superpower

Gen Z, having grown up in an era of rapid technological advancements and cultural shifts, has an inherent advantage in developing EQ. Their digital upbringing has given them exposure to diverse viewpoints, making them naturally adaptable and socially conscious. By sharpening their emotional intelligence, they can become the driving force behind more inclusive, innovative, and emotionally intelligent workplaces.

EQ: A Competitive Edge in the Modern Workplace

Technical skills may get your foot in the door, but EQ is what opens new opportunities, strengthens workplace relationships, and fuels long-term career success. Employers increasingly value emotional intelligence in candidates, recognizing that it leads to better teamwork, improved decision-making, and higher workplace morale.

EQ and Mental Well-Being: The Intersection of Success and Happiness

EQ isn't just about excelling at work—it's also about leading a fulfilling and balanced life. A well-developed emotional intelligence helps individuals manage stress, build resilience, and maintain healthy relationships, contributing to both personal and professional well-being.

Practical Exercises for Strengthening EQ

To develop your EQ, incorporate these hands-on exercises into your routine:

♦ **Daily Emotional Journaling:** Record your emotions, reactions, and thoughts to identify patterns and areas for improvement.

♦ **Active Listening Challenges:** Make a conscious effort to fully engage in conversations, avoiding distractions and focusing on the speaker's words and emotions.

♦ **Empathy Workouts:** Try stepping into someone else's shoes—consider their motivations, fears, and perspectives in different situations.

♦ **360-Degree Feedback:** Seek honest feedback from mentors, colleagues, and friends to uncover strengths and areas for growth.

Why People Become Unhappy at Work (and How Emotional Intelligence Helps)

In today's diverse and fast-paced workplaces, unhappiness often stems from emotional challenges rather than just workload or salary. Here's how emotional intelligence (EQ) can help Gen Z and beyond navigate workplace struggles:

1. Unrealistic Expectations → Adaptability

    ⊙ Expecting quick promotions or constant praise can lead to frustration.

    ⊙ EQ helps you manage expectations and embrace growth over time.

2. Lack of Purpose → Meaningful Work

    ⊙ Feeling stuck in a job with no impact can be demotivating.

    ⊙ EQ enables you to align your role with personal values and find fulfillment.

3. Comparing Yourself to Others → Self-Awareness

    ⊙ Seeing colleagues succeed faster can trigger self-doubt.

    ⊙ EQ teaches you to focus on your own progress and strengths.

4.   Workplace Conflicts → Relationship Management

⊙   Miscommunication and misunderstandings create tension.

⊙   EQ fosters empathy, active listening, and constructive conversations.

5.   Self-Doubt & Negative Self-Talk → Self-Confidence

⊙   Constantly feeling like an imposter affects motivation.

⊙   EQ helps you recognize achievements and build resilience.

6.   Burnout & Stress → Emotional Regulation

⊙   Overworking and ignoring mental health leads to exhaustion.

⊙   EQ promotes balance, stress management, and self-care.

7.   Lack of Recognition → Gratitude & Perspective

⊙   Feeling undervalued can make work seem meaningless.

⊙   EQ encourages appreciation for small wins and workplace contributions.

8.   Fear of Change → Growth Mindset

⊙   Uncertainty about new roles or responsibilities can be overwhelming.

⊙   EQ helps you embrace change as an opportunity rather than a threat.

By strengthening emotional intelligence, Gen Z professionals can navigate workplace challenges with confidence, connection, and clarity—leading to greater job satisfaction and long-term success.

Here's a pie chart visualizing the emotional challenges in the workplace and how emotional intelligence helps address them.

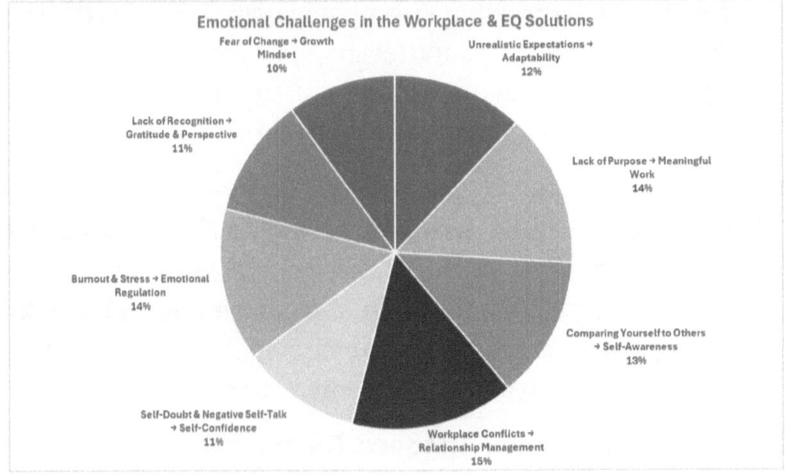

The Lifelong Journey of Emotional Growth

Emotional intelligence is not a one-time achievement but a lifelong skill that evolves with continuous practice and self-awareness. By embracing the power of EQ, professionals can foster stronger relationships, navigate workplace challenges with confidence, and create inclusive environments where everyone thrives. The future of work belongs to those who cannot only think critically but also connect emotionally—and EQ 2.0 is the roadmap to making that future a reality.

Actionable Exercises:

1. **Practice Active Listening:** For one day, focus on actively listening in every conversation. Make sure you maintain eye contact (or show attentiveness in virtual settings), let people finish their thoughts before you respond, and then summarize what they said to ensure you understood correctly. At the end of the day, think about how this changed the quality of your conversations.

2. **Create an Empathy Map:** Choose a colleague or team member you interact with regularly. Try to understand their perspective by creating an empathy map. Ask yourself what they might be thinking and feeling, what pressures they might be under, and what motivates them. Use this understanding to guide your next interaction with them.

3. **Role-Play Cultural Sensitivity:** Partner with a friend or colleague and practice having difficult workplace conversations that involve diverse cultural perspectives. Take turns playing different roles and focus on responding with empathy and respect. This exercise will help you develop your ability to navigate diverse interactions.

4. **Identify Emotional Triggers:** For the next week, keep a journal of situations that trigger strong emotional reactions. For each situation, write down what happened, how you felt, and how you responded. At the end of the week, look for patterns and think about how you can manage these emotions more effectively in the future.

5. **Take an Emotional Intelligence Assessment:** Find an online emotional intelligence assessment and take it. Use the results to identify your strengths and areas for improvement. Choose one specific area, like self-awareness or empathy, and set a goal to develop it further.

Key Takeaways:

1. **Self-Awareness is Foundational:** Understanding your own emotions and triggers is the first step to developing emotional intelligence.

2. **Self-Management is Key:** Learning to regulate your emotions and respond thoughtfully is crucial for navigating workplace challenges.

3. **Social Awareness Builds Connection:** Being able to read and understand the emotions of others fosters empathy and strengthens relationships.

4. **Relationship Management Drives Collaboration:** Cultivating strong relationships through effective communication and conflict resolution is essential for teamwork.

5. **EQ is a Competitive Advantage:** Emotional intelligence is increasingly valued in the workplace and can lead to better career opportunities.

6. **Diversity Requires Empathy:** Navigating diverse workplaces requires understanding and respecting different cultural perspectives.

7. **Emotional Intelligence Improves Well-being:** Developing EQ can help manage stress, build resilience, and contribute to overall happiness.

8. **Active Listening is Essential:** Truly listening to others and understanding their perspectives is key to building strong relationships.

9. **Feedback is a Tool for Growth:** Seeking and incorporating feedback from others can help you improve your emotional intelligence.

10. **EQ is a Lifelong Journey:** Emotional intelligence is a skill that requires continuous practice and development.

Chapter 5

THE GEN Z LEADER: BUILDING TRUST AND INSPIRING OTHERS EARLY IN YOUR CAREER

The traditional model of leadership, characterized by hierarchical structures and top-down authority, is rapidly becoming obsolete. In its place, a new paradigm is emerging, driven by collaboration, authenticity, and purpose. Gen Z, with its inherent understanding of the digital landscape and its commitment to social impact, is uniquely positioned to lead this transformation. This shift aligns perfectly with Simon Sinek's assertion that "Leadership is not about being in charge. Leadership is about taking care of those in your charge." Gen Z's focus on inclusivity and genuine connection naturally fosters this type of servant leadership. Therefore, this comprehensive guide provides a roadmap for young professionals to navigate the complexities of the modern workplace, build trust, inspire teams, and establish themselves as effective leaders from the earliest stages of their careers, emphasizing the importance of caring for and empowering their teams.

Leading with Authenticity and Purpose: The Foundation of Gen Z Leadership

Gen Z is a generation driven by purpose. Work is no longer simply a means to an end; it must align with personal values and contribute to something larger than oneself. Authentic leaders understand this and leverage it to create highly engaged and motivated teams. This involves:

80

- **Value-Driven Leadership:** Identify your core values and let them guide your decisions and actions. When your leadership is rooted in genuine beliefs, it resonates with others and inspires them to follow. Clearly articulate how the team's work connects to the organization's mission and its broader impact on the world.

- **Transparency and Vulnerability:** Building Trust in a Skeptical World: In an era of information overload, transparency is paramount. Be open and honest about your challenges, limitations, and learning process. Vulnerability is not a weakness; it's a strength. Admitting mistakes and seeking input from others fosters trust and creates a safe space for innovation.

- **The Power of Reverse Mentorship:** Bridging Generational Gaps: Gen Z possesses a unique understanding of technology, social media, and emerging trends. Offer your expertise to senior colleagues through reverse mentorship programs. This not only provides valuable insights but also demonstrates your leadership potential and fosters intergenerational collaboration.

Regularly communicate the impact of your team's work. Share success stories, highlight individual contributions, and connect daily tasks to the overall mission. This reinforces the sense of purpose and motivates team members to excel.

Leading with authenticity and purpose is increasingly vital, especially for engaging younger generations. Companies like Patagonia exemplify value-driven leadership. Founder Yvon Chouinard's decision to transfer ownership to combat climate change, even at the expense of potential profits, demonstrates a profound commitment to core values. This resonates strongly with Gen Z and Millennials, who prioritize purpose in their employment choices. Research consistently shows that companies with a clear sense of purpose experience higher employee satisfaction and retention rates.

Transparency and vulnerability are crucial components of effective leadership. Buffer, a social media management company, has built its reputation on radical openness, sharing everything from salary formulas to financial challenges. This level of transparency fosters trust, particularly in an era where information is often manipulated. Furthermore, research on psychological safety highlights that vulnerability creates a more trusting and innovative work environment. When leaders admit mistakes, it empowers others to do the same, fostering a culture of learning and growth.

Reverse mentorship is another powerful tool for modern leaders. Programs like Adobe's, where younger employees mentor senior leaders on digital trends, help bridge generational gaps and keep leaders up to date. These programs also empower younger employees, giving them a voice and developing their leadership skills. The increasing adoption of reverse mentorship reflects a broader recognition of the value of diverse perspectives in a rapidly changing business landscape.

Finally, consistently communicating the impact of individual work is essential for employee motivation and engagement. Studies underscore the importance of connecting individual contributions to the organization's overall mission. When employees understand how their work contributes to larger goals, they are more motivated and engaged. This can be achieved through internal newsletters, employee engagement surveys, and other forms of regular communication that highlight the collective impact of the workforce.

Cultivating Adaptability and Emotional Intelligence: Essential Skills for the Modern Leader

The modern workplace is characterized by constant change and disruption. Leaders must be adaptable, resilient, and emotionally intelligent to navigate this complex landscape. This requires:

- **Embracing a Growth Mindset:** Turning Challenges into Opportunities: Cultivate a mindset that views challenges as opportunities for growth and development. Encourage experimentation, celebrate learning from failures, and foster a culture of continuous improvement within your team.

♦ **Harnessing Emotional Intelligence:** Connecting with Your Team on a Human Level: Emotional intelligence (EQ) is the ability to understand and manage your own emotions and those of others. Develop self-awareness, practice empathy, and hone your communication skills to build strong relationships and create a supportive team environment.

♦ **The Art of Storytelling:** Inspiring Action Through Narrative: Stories have the power to connect with people on an emotional level. Use storytelling to communicate your vision, inspire your team, and make complex ideas more accessible. Craft compelling narratives that resonate with your audience and motivate them to action.

♦ **Navigating a Non-Linear Career Path:** Embracing the Ecosystem Mindset: Career paths are no longer linear progressions. Embrace a more fluid approach, focusing on skill development, diverse experiences, and building a strong professional network. View your career as an ecosystem, where you can learn, grow, and contribute in many ways.

Practice active listening. Pay attention to both the verbal and nonverbal cues of your team members. Ask clarifying questions and summarize what you've heard to ensure understanding. This demonstrates that you value their input and fosters open communication.

Satya Nadella's transformation of Microsoft

Satya Nadella, upon becoming CEO of Microsoft in 2014, inherited a company grappling with a rapidly shifting tech landscape and internal cultural challenges. Microsoft, once a dominant force, was perceived as rigid, slow to innovate, and internally competitive. Nadella's approach embodied the very principles outlined. He fostered a growth mindset by shifting the company's focus from a "know-it-all" culture to a "learn-it-all" one. He encouraged experimentation, even with projects that might fail, and celebrated learning from those experiences. This was evident in Microsoft's renewed focus on cloud computing and AI, areas where they had previously lagged.

Nadella also prioritized emotional intelligence. He emphasized empathy, not just within the company but also in how Microsoft interacted with its customers and partners. He focused on building bridges, repairing strained relationships, and creating a more collaborative environment. His approach was evident in his willingness to acknowledge past mistakes and his focus on empowering employees. Furthermore, Nadella's ability to communicate a clear vision through compelling narratives was crucial. He articulated a vision of Microsoft as a company that empowered every person and organization on the planet to achieve more, a narrative that resonated with employees and customers alike. This storytelling helped to shift the company's image and inspire renewed enthusiasm.

Finally, Nadella's own career path exemplifies navigating a non-linear journey. He didn't follow a traditional, predictable trajectory to the top. Instead, he embraced diverse experiences, focusing on continuous learning and building a strong network. His leadership reflected an "ecosystem mindset," recognizing the interconnectedness of various aspects of the business and the importance of adaptability. Throughout his tenure, Nadella's active listening was apparent. He consistently sought feedback, engaged in open dialogue, and demonstrated a genuine interest in understanding the perspectives of his employees and partners. This approach helped to build trust and foster a more collaborative work environment.

Nadella's transformation of Microsoft demonstrates that cultivating adaptability, emotional intelligence, and a growth mindset are not just theoretical concepts but essential skills for navigating the complexities of the modern workplace.

Building Trust Through Relatability and Inclusivity: Creating a Culture of Belonging

Trust is the cornerstone of effective leadership. Gen Z leaders can build trust by being relatable, authentic, and committed to creating inclusive environments. This involves:

- **Relatability - Connecting with Your Team on a Personal Level:** Share your own experiences, challenges, and vulnerabilities. Be approachable and create opportunities for open dialogue. When you connect with your team on a personal level, you build stronger relationships and foster a sense of camaraderie.

- **Inclusivity - Creating a Space Where Everyone Thrives:** Champion diversity and inclusion in all its forms. Create a culture where everyone feels valued, respected, and empowered to contribute their unique perspectives. Actively seek out diverse voices and ensure that all team members have equal opportunities to succeed.

- **Hyper-Connectivity - Leveraging Digital Platforms for Influence:** Utilize social media and other digital platforms to connect with your team, share knowledge, and build your professional network. Engage in meaningful conversations, contribute valuable content, and establish yourself as a thought leader in your field.

Create a safe space for feedback. Encourage team members to share their thoughts and ideas without fear of judgment. Actively listen to their concerns and take action to address them. This demonstrates that you value their input and are committed to creating a positive work environment.

A Bold First Step

Ryan, fresh out of business school, landed a role at a legacy logistics firm, a place known for its rigid hierarchy and dwindling morale. He quickly sensed a disconnect; employees felt like cogs in a machine, their voices unheard.

Instead of accepting the status quo, Ryan decided to leverage his relatability. He didn't approach his manager with a grand, corporate proposal. Instead, he shared his own feelings of initial disorientation and a desire to understand the team better. "I felt like I was learning in the dark," he admitted, "and I wondered if others felt the same." This vulnerability resonated with his manager, who allowed him to pilot a "Pulse Check" – an anonymous feedback system.

Ryan didn't just collect data; he made it inclusive. He ensured the feedback platform was accessible to everyone, regardless of their tech comfort level, and actively sought input from diverse team members, including those often overlooked. He even translated some feedback into simpler terms for those who found the corporate jargon confusing.

He then used hyper-connectivity to his advantage. He created a dedicated online channel (a simple group chat) where he shared summarized feedback and proposed solutions. He didn't just post; he engaged in conversations, answering questions and addressing concerns. He even used short, informal videos to explain complex issues, making them more digestible.

In team meetings, Ryan shared his own experiences of facing similar challenges, building relatability. "I know how frustrating it is when workflows are unclear," he'd say, "I've been there." He highlighted the importance of peer-recognition, not just from management, and championed the idea of a digital "kudos board" to celebrate contributions, fostering a sense of inclusivity and appreciation.

Ryan didn't just suggest changes; he took ownership, even though it wasn't strictly his job. He personally helped streamline workflows and set up the digital recognition board, demonstrating his commitment to action. He used the online channel to share updates and celebrate successes, creating a sense of shared progress.

The impact was tangible. Engagement scores rose, and the department became a model for the rest of the company. Ryan's initiative wasn't just about data; it was about building genuine connections, fostering a sense of belonging, and using digital tools to amplify voices.

Ryan, a Gen Z leader, demonstrated that building trust begins with relatability, creating inclusivity, and leveraging hyper-connectivity to amplify feedback and inspire change. His willingness to share his own experiences, champion diverse voices, and utilize digital platforms to connect made him a catalyst for a more engaged and connected workplace.

Mastering the Art of Communication: The Key to Effective Leadership

Communication is the lifeblood of any team. Effective leaders are skilled communicators, able to articulate their vision clearly, listen actively, and provide constructive feedback. Gen Z leaders can excel in communication by:

◆ **Empowering Through Inquiry:** Shifting from Telling to Asking: Move away from a command-and-control style of leadership and embrace a more collaborative approach. Ask questions, solicit input, and encourage your team to take ownership of their work.

◆ **The Power of Language:** Shaping Culture Through Words: Be mindful of the language you use. Choose words that are inclusive, empowering and promote a positive and collaborative culture. Avoid jargon and use clear, concise language that everyone can understand.

◆ **Creating Psychological Safety:** Fostering Open and Honest Dialogue: Psychological safety is the belief that you can speak up without fear of negative consequences. Create a team environment where everyone feels safe to share their ideas, ask questions, and even admit mistakes.

♦ **Active Listening:** The Foundation of Effective Communication: Pay attention not just to the words being spoken but also to the nonverbal cues. Listen to understand, not just to respond. Ask clarifying questions and summarize what you've heard to ensure that you've understood correctly.

Provide regular feedback to your team members. Be specific and constructive and focus on behaviors rather than personality traits. Offer both positive feedback and areas for improvement. This helps team members grow and develop their skills.

The rise of Brené Brown and her impact on leadership communication

Brené Brown, a research professor and author, has become a prominent figure in leadership development by emphasizing vulnerability, empathy, and honest communication. Her approach directly aligns with the points mentioned.

♦ **Empowering Through Inquiry:** Brown's research and teachings are rooted in asking questions and exploring human experiences. She doesn't dictate; she facilitates conversations, encouraging people to reflect on their own lives and leadership styles. Her podcast, "Unlocking Us," is built on deep conversations and asking the questions that most people are afraid to ask. This approach allows her audience to come to their own realizations, therefore taking ownership of their personal growth.

♦ **The Power of Language:** Brown is meticulous about the language she uses. She emphasizes the importance of choosing words that foster connection and understanding. She actively works to dismantle jargon and promotes clear, accessible communication. Her focus on words like "vulnerability," "empathy," and "courage" has shifted the conversation around leadership, making it more human-centered. She avoids language that promotes shame or blame.

- **Creating Psychological Safety:** Brown's work is all about creating a safe space for vulnerability. She encourages leaders to be authentic and to acknowledge their imperfections. By sharing her own vulnerabilities, she creates an environment where others feel safe to do the same. Her emphasis on empathy and understanding helps to build trust and foster open dialogue. When she speaks to groups, she creates an atmosphere that allows people to openly discuss difficult topics.

- **Active Listening:** Brown's interviews and presentations demonstrate her commitment to active listening. She pays close attention to the nuances of language and nonverbal cues. She often pauses to reflect on what others have said, asking clarifying questions and summarizing key points. Her ability to connect with her audience on an emotional level is a testament to her active listening skills.

- **Regular Feedback:** While Brown's primary focus isn't traditional performance feedback, she provides constant feedback through her research and storytelling. She highlights the importance of self-reflection and encourages people to examine their own behaviors. Her work provides a framework for understanding how our actions impact others, which is a form of continuous feedback. Her books and talks provide her audience with constructive feedback on how to improve their lives and leadership skills.

Brené Brown's work serves as a powerful example of how effective communication can transform leadership. Her emphasis on vulnerability, empathy, and honest dialogue has resonated with audiences around the world, demonstrating the power of these communication principles in action.

Influence Over Authority: Leading Through Action and Inspiration

In the modern workplace, influence is more valuable than authority. Gen Z leaders can build influence by demonstrating competence, acting with integrity, and inspiring others to follow. This involves:

- **Leading by Example:** Walking the Talk: Your actions speak louder than words. Demonstrate the behaviors and values that you expect from your team. Be a role model for hard work, dedication, and ethical conduct.

- **Clarity and Confidence:** Communicating Your Vision with Conviction: Communicate your vision clearly and confidently. Be decisive and articulate your ideas in a way that inspires trust and confidence.

- **Seeking and Providing Feedback:** Fostering a Culture of Continuous Improvement: Create a culture where feedback is valued and encouraged. Seek feedback from your team members and provide them with constructive criticism to help them grow and develop.

- **Focusing on the "Why":** Connecting Work to a Larger Purpose: Help your team understand the bigger picture. Explain how their work contributes to the organization's overall goals and its impact on the world. This gives their work meaning and motivates them to perform at their best.

Become a problem-solver. Identify challenges and proactively offer solutions. This demonstrates initiative and positions you as a valuable asset to your team and organization.

Sasha's Influential Data Dive

Sasha, a 24-year-old data analyst, joined a fast-paced tech startup with a flat organizational structure. Her first major project involved analyzing customer behavior for a crucial product launch, requiring collaboration with a diverse and experienced cross-functional team.

Initially, Sasha faced skepticism. Some team members, accustomed to traditional hierarchies, dismissed her ideas, assuming her youth meant a lack of expertise. Instead of asserting authority she didn't have, Sasha decided to lead by example. She demonstrated humility by actively listening to their concerns and integrity by acknowledging their expertise.

She scheduled one-on-one meetings, not to dictate, but to learn. She asked insightful questions, focusing on their challenges and objectives, showing a genuine interest in their perspectives. This seeking feedback from her peers, even before giving any, was a key move.

When Sasha reconvened the team, she presented her analysis with clarity and confidence. She didn't just dump raw data; she told a story, painting a clear picture of customer behavior. She articulated her vision for the product launch, connecting the data to the team's shared goal. She focused on the "why", explaining how their combined efforts would directly impact customer satisfaction and the company's success.

She also demonstrated influence over authority by highlighting each team member's unique contributions. "Your insights into user interface design perfectly align with this data trend," she said, "and your marketing strategies directly address these customer pain points. How can we integrate these strengths more effectively?" This approach fostered a sense of collaboration and showed that she valued their expertise. She was also providing feedback by aligning their work with the data but doing so in a constructive and positive manner.

Sasha also proactively addressed potential problems. When she noticed a communication gap between the design and development teams, she suggested a shared digital whiteboard, demonstrating her problem-solving skills. She then led a brief tutorial on how to use it, leading by example and fostering a culture of continuous improvement.

Her ability to unite the team under a shared vision, combined with her data-driven insights and collaborative approach, earned her their respect. The project was a resounding success, and within a year, Sasha was promoted. She proved that leadership wasn't about authority; it was about influence built on trust, competence, and a shared sense of purpose.

Sasha, a Gen Z leader, demonstrated that in a modern workplace, influence over authority is paramount. By leading by example, communicating with clarity and confidence, seeking and providing feedback, and focusing on the "why", she inspired her team and achieved remarkable results.

Tips for Gen Z leaders:

Gen Z leaders are stepping into the workforce with a unique set of values and expectations. To thrive and inspire others early in your career, focus on these key principles:

Be Authentic and Transparent: Gen Z values authenticity. Don't try to be someone you're not. Be genuine in your interactions, share your own experiences (including failures!), and be transparent about your decision-making processes. This builds trust and fosters a sense of connection with your team. Early in your career, this might mean admitting when you don't know something and being open about your learning journey.

Embrace Technology: Gen Z is digitally native. Leverage technology not just for efficiency, but also for communication, collaboration, and innovation. Explore new tools and platforms to connect with your team, streamline workflows, and create engaging experiences. As a young leader, your tech-savviness can be a real asset.

Provide Purpose and Meaning: Gen Z seeks purpose in their work. Connect individual tasks to the bigger picture and explain how each team member contributes to the overall mission. Highlight the positive impact of their work and create opportunities for them to engage with projects that align with their values. Early on, demonstrating how your team's work connects to a larger purpose will be incredibly motivating.

Offer Flexibility and Autonomy: Gen Z values work-life integration and autonomy. Offer flexible work arrangements where possible, empower team members to make decisions, and give them ownership over their projects. This demonstrates trust and allows individuals to work in ways that maximize their productivity and well-being. Even early in your leadership journey, advocating for flexibility within your team can be impactful.

Foster a Culture of Learning and Growth: Gen Z is eager to learn and develop new skills. Create opportunities for professional development, mentorship, and cross-training. Encourage continuous learning and provide resources to support their growth. As a young leader, your own commitment to learning will set a positive example.

Give Regular Feedback and Recognition: Gen Z appreciates regular feedback, both positive and constructive. Provide frequent check-ins, offer specific and actionable feedback, and recognize accomplishments, both big and small. Early in your career, developing a habit of providing regular feedback will make you a more effective leader.

Promote Diversity and Inclusion: Gen Z is the most diverse generation yet and values inclusivity. Create a welcoming and inclusive environment where everyone feels respected, valued, and heard. Actively promote diversity in your team and challenge any form of discrimination or bias. Early in your career, being a champion for diversity and inclusion will set you apart.

Communicate Clearly and Directly: Gen Z prefers clear, concise, and direct communication. Avoid jargon and be transparent in your messaging. Utilize various communication channels to ensure your message is received and understood. As a young leader, mastering clear communication is essential for building trust and avoiding misunderstandings.

Be Open to Feedback and Ideas: Gen Z wants to be heard. Create a culture where team members feel comfortable sharing their ideas and providing feedback, even if it's critical. Actively listen to their perspectives and be open to incorporating their suggestions. Early on, demonstrating that you value their input will empower your team.

Lead with Empathy and Understanding: Gen Z values emotional intelligence and empathy. Take the time to understand your team members' perspectives, acknowledge their feelings, and show compassion. Create a supportive and caring environment where they feel comfortable being themselves. Leading with empathy, even early in your career, will create a stronger and more connected team.

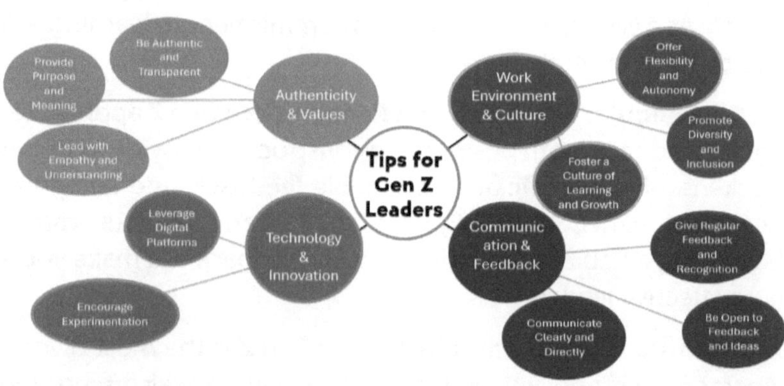

Embracing the Future of Leadership

Gen Z is poised to redefine leadership for the 21st century. By embracing authenticity, adaptability, inclusivity, and a collaborative approach, young professionals can build trust, inspire teams, and create positive change in the world. Instead of passively waiting for the future, Gen Z is actively shaping it, embodying Peter Drucker's wisdom: "The best way to predict the future is to create it." This generation understands that the future of leadership is not about power or authority; it's about influence, impact, and the ability to empower others to achieve their full potential. Therefore, embrace your unique strengths, cultivate the skills outlined in this book, and become the leader you aspire to be, actively crafting the leadership landscape of tomorrow.

Actionable Exercises:

1. **Define Your Leadership Values:** Take a moment to write down three core values that are important to you as a leader. Think about how these values affect your daily actions and find ways to consistently show them in your interactions with others. This will help you lead with more intention.

2. **Build Your Trust Bank:** Choose three small actions you can take this week to build trust with your colleagues. This could be meeting a deadline, offering help, or admitting a mistake. Keep track of what happens and see how these actions affect your relationships.

3. **Inspire Through Storytelling:** Practice sharing a personal story about a challenge you overcame, a lesson you learned, or a moment of growth. Share this story in a meeting or conversation to connect with and inspire others. Stories are powerful tools for building connections.

4. **Seek Feedback to Grow:** Ask a mentor, manager, or peer for feedback on your leadership potential. Ask questions like, "What's one thing I do that builds trust?" and "What's one area I could improve?" Use this feedback to set a goal for your personal development.

5. **Practice Inclusive Decision-Making:** The next time you're in a group setting, make a conscious effort to seek input from quieter team members or those with different perspectives. Think about how this approach changes the team's dynamic and morale.

Key Takeaways:

1. **Authenticity and Purpose are Key:** Gen Z leaders should lead with genuine values and connect their work to a larger purpose.

2. **Transparency Builds Trust:** Being open and honest about challenges and limitations fosters trust and creates a safe environment.

3. **Emotional Intelligence is Essential:** Understanding and managing emotions, both your own and others', is crucial for effective leadership.

4. **Storytelling Inspires Action:** Using narratives to communicate vision and connect with people emotionally is a powerful leadership tool.

5. **Relatability Creates Connection:** Sharing personal experiences and vulnerabilities builds stronger relationships and fosters camaraderie.

6. **Inclusivity Drives Success:** Championing diversity and creating a culture where everyone feels valued is essential for a thriving team.

7. **Communication is Vital:** Effective leaders are skilled communicators who listen actively and provide clear feedback.

8. **Influence Trumps Authority:** Building influence through competence and integrity is more valuable than relying on authority.

9. **Continuous Learning is Crucial:** Embracing a growth mindset and fostering a culture of learning is essential in the modern workplace.

10. **Leading by Example Sets the Tone:** Demonstrating the behaviors and values you expect from others is the most effective way to lead.

Chapter 6

THE COLLABORATION EDGE: WINNING AS A TEAM IN REMOTE AND HYBRID WORKPLACES

Forget the old image of work – the rigid 9-to-5, the stuffy office, the endless commute. For Gen Z, the future of work is already here, and it's defined by flexibility, purpose, and connection. Remote and hybrid models have become the norm, offering incredible freedom but also a unique set of challenges. How do you build trust and camaraderie when your teammates are scattered across time zones? How do you communicate effectively when most interactions happen through screens? As Henry Ford wisely stated, "Coming together is a beginning, keeping together is progress, working together is success." In the context of remote and hybrid work, this highlights the necessity of actively fostering connection beyond mere digital presence. It's not just about the tools; it's about the deliberate effort to build and maintain a cohesive team culture, even when physically separated. This chapter is your guide to navigating this new landscape, equipping you with the skills and strategies to not just survive, but thrive in the world of remote and hybrid work, focusing on how to achieve that 'working together' success.

The Changing Landscape of Teamwork

The workplace has undergone a dramatic transformation. We've traded watercooler conversations for video calls and in-person brainstorming sessions for shared online documents. This shift has unlocked incredible possibilities – greater flexibility, a wider talent pool, and the potential for a better work-life balance. But it also presents a paradox: the more tools we have to connect, the harder it can be to forge genuine connections.

This is the collaboration edge – the ability to build high-performing teams in a world where work happens anytime, anywhere. It's about more than just mastering the technology; it's about cultivating a new mindset, one that prioritizes empathy, communication, and a shared sense of purpose.

The Gen Z Advantage

As digital natives, Gen Z is uniquely positioned to excel in this new world of work. You're tech-savvy, adaptable, and comfortable with virtual communication. But to truly thrive, you need to go beyond the tools. This means:

- **Intentional Communication:** Mastering the nuances of digital communication to build trust and avoid misunderstandings.

- **Cultural Sensitivity:** Navigating diverse perspectives and communication styles in a globalized workforce.

- **Relationship Building:** Creating genuine connections with colleagues, even when you've never met them in person.

This chapter will delve into these skills and more, providing you with the knowledge and tools you need to become a collaboration champion.

Building Trust and Psychological Safety

The Foundation of Virtual Teams

Trust is the bedrock of any successful team, but in remote and hybrid environments, it takes on even greater importance. Without the casual interactions of a shared office, it's easy to feel disconnected and isolated. Building trust requires a conscious effort, a willingness to be vulnerable, and a commitment to open communication.

Here's how to cultivate trust in a virtual world:

- **Overcommunicate (without overwhelming):** Keep your team informed about your progress, challenges, and any roadblocks you encounter. Regular updates, even brief ones, can go a long way in building trust and transparency.

- **Embrace transparency:** Share your goals, priorities, and even your struggles. When teams have a clear understanding of what everyone is working on, they're more likely to support each other and collaborate effectively.

- **Show your human side:** Don't let virtual interactions become purely transactional. Take time to connect with your colleagues on a personal level – share a funny anecdote, talk about your weekend plans, or simply ask how they're doing.

- **Deliver on your promises:** Reliability is paramount in remote teams. If you commit to something, follow through. Your actions speak louder than words and consistently meeting your commitments will build trust and respect.

Creating a Safe Space for Collaboration

Psychological safety is the secret weapon of high-performing teams. It's the feeling that you can speak your mind, ask questions, and take risks without fear of judgment or ridicule. In a virtual environment, where it's easier to feel isolated and insecure, psychological safety is essential for fostering open communication and encouraging innovation.

Here's how to cultivate psychological safety in your team:

♦ **Encourage open dialogue:** Create a space where everyone feels comfortable sharing their ideas and opinions, even if they differ from the majority.

♦ **Normalize learning from mistakes:** Mistakes are inevitable, especially when trying new things. Encourage a growth mindset where mistakes are seen as opportunities for learning and improvement.

♦ **Ensure all voices are heard:** Don't let meetings be dominated by the loudest voices. Actively solicit input from quieter team members and create opportunities for everyone to contribute.

A Marketing Team Launching a New Digital Campaign Remotely

The Team: A marketing team of 8, spread across three different time zones, is tasked with launching a new digital campaign for a tech startup. They've been working remotely for over a year.

The Challenge: The team is facing a tight deadline and encountering unexpected technical glitches with their chosen marketing automation platform. This is causing delays and frustration.

How the Team Applied the Principles:

Overcommunicate (without overwhelming): The project manager, Anita, established a daily 15-minute "stand-up" video call. During these calls, each team member shared their progress, any roadblocks they encountered, and their priorities for the day. She also used a dedicated Slack channel for real-time updates and quick questions, ensuring everyone was kept in the loop without constant, lengthy emails. When the technical glitches arose, Anita immediately informed the team, outlining the issue and the steps being taken to resolve it, rather than hiding the problem.

Embrace transparency: During a virtual meeting, the team lead, David, openly admitted that they had underestimated the complexity of integrating the new automation platform. He shared the revised project timeline and explained the reasons for the delay, fostering a sense of shared understanding. The team used a shared project management tool, where everyone could see the progress of each task.

Show your human side: During the stand-up calls, team members would often share a brief personal anecdote or ask about each other's weekends. When one team member, Emily, mentioned she was feeling overwhelmed, Anita offered to schedule a one-on-one call to brainstorm solutions and provide support. The team would have a virtual "coffee break" once a week, where they would talk about non-work related topics.

Deliver on your promises: When a team member, John, volunteered to research alternative solutions to the technical glitches, he delivered a comprehensive report within the agreed-upon timeframe. Anita consistently followed up on action items and provided timely feedback, demonstrating her reliability.

Encourage open dialogue: During brainstorming sessions, the team used virtual whiteboards to capture everyone's ideas. Anita actively encouraged team members to share their thoughts, even if they were unconventional.

Normalize learning from mistakes: When a team member, Mark, accidentally sent out an incomplete version of the campaign email, David addressed the issue in a calm and constructive manner. Instead of assigning blame, he focused on identifying the root cause and implementing safeguards to prevent future errors. The team held a short meeting to discuss what they learned from the mistake.

Ensure all voices are heard: Anita used the chat function during virtual meetings to encourage quieter team members to share their thoughts. She also implemented a "round-robin" approach, where each team member had the opportunity to speak in turn. She would follow up with team members that were quiet, after the meetings, to see if they had any additional thoughts.

Outcome: Despite the initial challenges, the marketing team successfully launched the campaign on time. The open communication, transparency, and psychological safety fostered by the team lead and project manager created a supportive and collaborative environment, enabling the team to overcome obstacles and achieve their goals. The team also learned valuable lessons about the new marketing platform.

The New Language of Work

In a world where most interactions happen through screens, mastering digital communication is no longer optional – it's essential. The subtle cues we rely on in face-to-face conversations, like tone of voice and body language, are often lost in the digital world, leading to misinterpretations and misunderstandings.

To become a digital communication pro, focus on these key skills:

- **Clarity over brevity:** While concise communication is important, clarity should be your top priority. Avoid vague messages that can lead to confusion. Instead of a simple "OK," try "Thanks for the update! I'll review it and get back to you by tomorrow."

- **Emojis and punctuation with purpose:** Emojis and punctuation can add nuance and personality to your messages but use them thoughtfully. A well-placed emoji can convey warmth and enthusiasm but overdoing it can make you seem unprofessional.

◆ **Speed matters:** Responding promptly to messages shows that you're engaged and reliable. Delays, on the other hand, can cause frustration and erode trust.

◆ **Choose the right medium:** Not every conversation requires a video call. Sometimes a well-structured email or a quick voice note is more efficient and effective.

Setting Communication Ground Rules

To avoid communication breakdowns, establish clear norms with your team:

◆ **Response times:** Agree on expected response times for messages and emails.

◆ **Preferred platforms:** Determine which platforms are best suited for different types of communication (e.g., quick questions on Slack, in-depth discussions via email).

◆ **Meeting etiquette:** Establish guidelines for virtual meetings, such as whether cameras should be on or off, how to handle interruptions, and how to ensure everyone has a chance to speak.

The New Rules of Productivity:

Ditching the 9-to-5 Grind

The traditional 9-to-5 workday is a relic of the past. Gen Z values flexibility, and research shows that employees who have control over their work schedule are often more productive and engaged. The key to unlocking this productivity boost is embracing asynchronous work.

The Power of Asynchronous Work

Asynchronous work means that not everyone needs to be online at the same time. Instead of relying on synchronous meetings for every discussion, teams can leverage project management tools, shared documents, and other asynchronous communication channels to keep projects moving forward.

Here are some productivity hacks for the remote world:

♦ **Time blocking:** Schedule dedicated blocks of time for focused work, meetings, and breaks. This helps you prioritize tasks and avoid distractions.

♦ **The two-minute rule:** If a task takes less than two minutes to complete, do it immediately. This prevents small tasks from piling up and overwhelming you.

♦ **Collaboration tools:** Master the art of using collaboration tools like Notion, Trello, and Slack to streamline teamwork, track progress, and keep everyone on the same page.

Virtual Leadership: Leading from Anywhere

The Evolving Role of the Leader

In a remote or hybrid environment, leadership is less about command and control and more about empowerment and enablement. Effective leaders create a clear vision, foster a culture of trust, and provide the support their team needs to succeed.

Here are the hallmarks of great remote leaders:

♦ **Clear vision and goals:** Communicate a clear vision for the team and set specific, measurable goals. In the absence of a shared physical space, clarity is crucial.

♦ **Empathy and emotional intelligence:** Recognize that remote work presents unique challenges and be sensitive to the diverse needs of your team members.

♦ **Proactive engagement:** Don't wait for problems to arise. Anticipate challenges and address them proactively. Regularly check in with your team, both individually and as a group.

Leading Without a Title

Even if you're not in a formal management position, you can still demonstrate leadership in a remote setting:

- **Take initiative:** Don't just identify problems – offer solutions.

- **Be a connector:** Facilitate collaboration and help your teammates build relationships with each other.

- **Share knowledge:** Create a culture of learning by sharing your expertise and helping others develop their skills.

The Future of Collaboration

Remote and hybrid work are here to stay, and the way we collaborate will continue to evolve. Companies that prioritize strong digital cultures, flexible work arrangements, and innovative collaboration tools will be best positioned to attract and retain top talent. For Gen Z, key takeaways include the paramount importance of trust, built through transparency, reliability, and genuine human connection; mastering digital communication by communicating clearly, being responsive, and choosing the right medium; focusing on results over hours worked, embracing asynchronous work, and leveraging collaboration tools; recognizing that leadership is for everyone, regardless of formal position; and embracing change by staying adaptable and constantly learning. By mastering these principles, Gen Z professionals can not only thrive in the new world of work but also shape its future. The collaboration edge is yours – use it to build a fulfilling and impactful career.

The Virtual Watercooler Revolution

When the pandemic forced her company to switch to remote work, Priya, a product manager, noticed that her team's camaraderie began to deteriorate. Meetings were strictly task-focused, and informal conversations—the glue of team dynamics—were fading.

Priya decided to experiment with a virtual "Watercooler Friday." Every Friday, the last 15 minutes of their team meeting were reserved for casual chats. To make it engage, she introduced themes like "Show and Tell" or "Guess the Baby Photo."

Initially, participation was lukewarm, with only a few team members joining in. But over time, the initiative gained momentum. During one session, a junior developer shared a personal story about moving countries alone, which resonated with others who had similar experiences. That moment of vulnerability deepened trust within the team.

As weeks passed, Priya observed noticeable changes. Collaboration improved, and team members were more willing to ask for help or share ideas during work discussions. The relaxed atmosphere carried over into their day-to-day interactions, leading to a 20% increase in project completion speed.

In remote and hybrid workplaces, fostering informal connections is as crucial as task management. Small initiatives can build trust, leading to stronger collaboration and better outcomes.

The Silent Hero of Time Zones

Carlos, a UX designer based in Mexico City, was part of a hybrid team spread across five time zones. Meetings were a logistical nightmare, with some teammates waking up at dawn while others stayed late into the night. Frustration grew as missed deadlines and miscommunications became frequent.

Carlos, despite not being the team lead, decided to step up. He analyzed the team's workflow and realized that most issues stemmed from poor handoffs. To address this, he introduced a "24-Hour Handoff" strategy:

1. **Shared Task Board:** Carlos created a shared Kanban board where everyone updated their progress at the end of their workday.

2. **Video Handoffs:** Instead of written updates, team members recorded short videos explaining their progress and any roadblocks.

3. **Clear Ownership:** He established a protocol for assigning clear next steps to the person starting their day next.

Within a month, the team's efficiency improved dramatically. Deadlines were met consistently, and the asynchronous handoffs reduced the need for real-time meetings. The team even voted Carlos as their "Collaboration MVP, Minimum Viable Product" recognizing his role in transforming their workflow.

In remote and hybrid settings, proactive solutions to logistical challenges can unite global teams, ensuring smooth collaboration despite time zone differences.

In conclusion, navigating the collaboration edge in remote and hybrid workplaces demands a shift in mindset and a commitment to new ways of working. From building trust and fostering psychological safety to mastering digital communication and embracing asynchronous work, the skills and strategies outlined in this chapter are essential for Gen Z professionals. As you embark on your career journey, remember that true success in this interconnected world is often found in empowering those around you. It is literally true that you can succeed best and quickest by helping others to succeed," - Napoleon Hill. By prioritizing collaboration, empathy, and a shared sense of purpose, you can not only thrive but also contribute to a more effective, inclusive, and fulfilling future of work.

Collaboration Wordcloud:

Actionable Exercises:

1. **Set Clear Team Goals:** Get together with your team and define three goals that you want to achieve in the next month. Make sure these goals are specific and that you can measure your progress. Break down each goal into smaller tasks and assign who is responsible for each. Make sure everyone understands how their work contributes to the team's success and how working together will help you reach those goals.

2. **Schedule a Virtual Team Check-In:** Set up a regular online meeting for your team to talk about how things are going,

what challenges you're facing, and what you've accomplished. Use this time to celebrate successes and work together to find solutions to any problems. Also, create a space for both work-related and personal updates to help everyone stay connected.

3. **Create a Collaboration Tool Cheat Sheet:** Make a guide that explains how to use the different online tools your team uses to work together remotely, like Slack, Zoom, or Google Drive. Outline the best ways to use each tool so that everyone knows how to use them effectively. Then, share this guide with your team.

4. **Role Clarity Exercise:** Have each person on your team write down what their specific role and responsibilities are. Then, have them share how their role helps the team achieve its overall goals. Use this to make sure everyone understands their role and how it fits into the bigger picture.

5. **Build a Virtual Team Culture:** Organize a fun online activity for your team, like a trivia game, a virtual coffee break, or a "show and tell" session. Choose activities that help people bond and feel like they belong to the team.

Key Takeaways:

1. **Trust is Essential:** Building trust through open communication, reliability, and showing your human side is critical for successful remote teams.

2. **Digital Communication Skills Matter:** Communicating clearly, being responsive, and choosing the right online tools are essential for avoiding misunderstandings.

3. **Flexibility Boosts Productivity:** Embracing flexible work schedules and asynchronous work can lead to increased productivity and engagement.

4. **Leadership is About Empowerment:** Effective remote leaders create a clear vision, foster trust, and support their team members.

5. **Everyone Can Lead:** You can demonstrate leadership in a remote setting by taking initiative, connecting teammates, and sharing your knowledge.

6. **Asynchronous Work is Powerful:** Leveraging tools and strategies to work effectively even when team members aren't online at the same time is key.

7. **Over-Communication is Key:** In remote settings, it's better to over-communicate important information to avoid confusion and ensure everyone is aligned.

8. **Adaptability is Crucial:** Being flexible with work hours, communication styles, and processes is important for navigating remote and hybrid work.

9. **Clear Expectations Prevent Issues:** Setting clear expectations around communication, availability, and deadlines helps prevent frustration and miscommunication.

10. **Informal Connections Matter:** Fostering informal connections and building a strong team culture are just as important as task management in remote work.

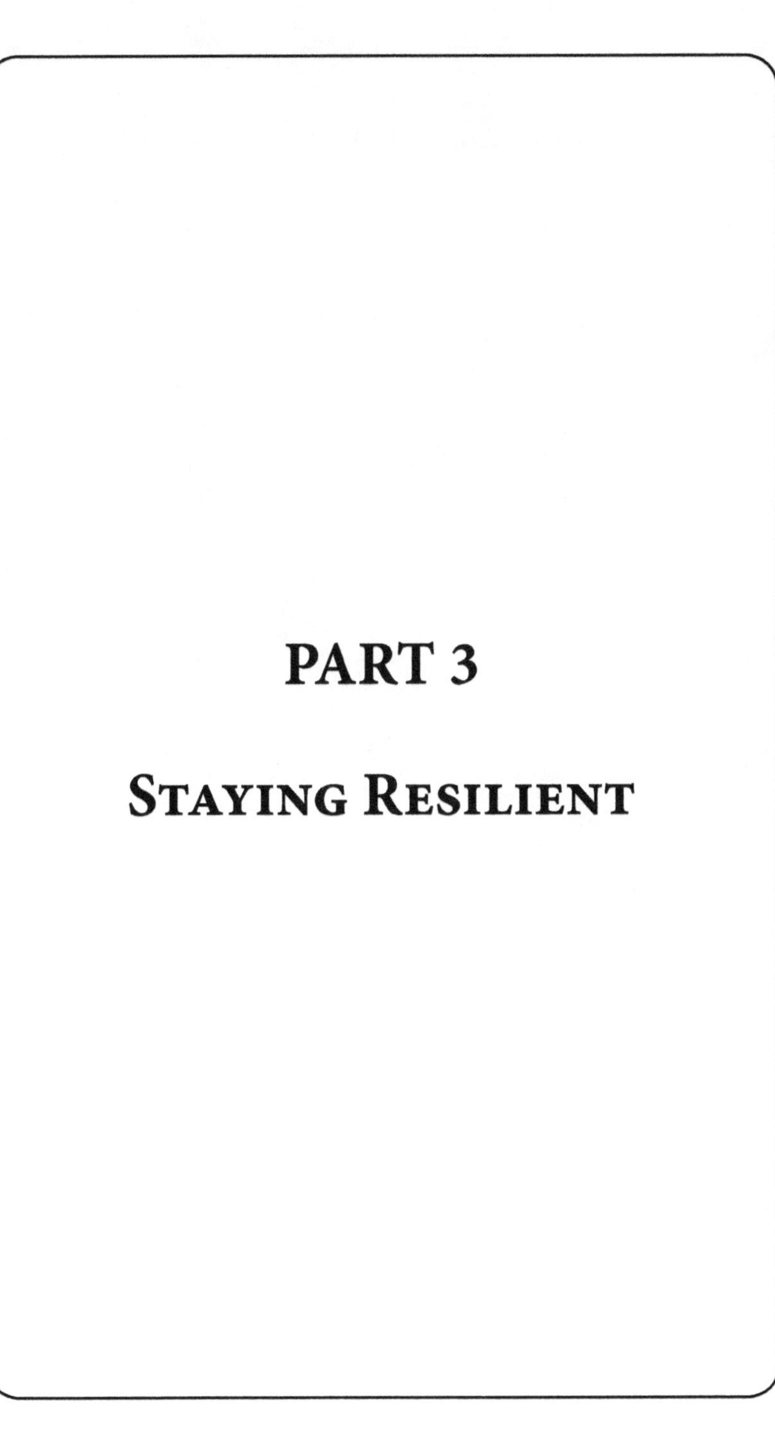

PART 3

STAYING RESILIENT

Chapter 7

ADAPTABILITY: THE SUPERPOWER FOR A RAPIDLY CHANGING WORLD

Gen Z is inheriting a world defined by constant flux: rapid technological evolution, volatile economic landscapes, and a barrage of unforeseen challenges. In this dynamic and unpredictable environment, adaptability transcends being a mere desirable trait; it's the quintessential superpower for navigating the 21st century and flourishing in the modern workplace. As Robert Greene aptly stated, 'The future belongs to those who learn more skills and combine them in creative ways.' This statement underscores the core principle of adaptability: It's not simply about reacting to change but proactively acquiring and integrating diverse skillsets to forge novel solutions. This chapter will delve into the essence of adaptability, dissecting its core components and providing actionable strategies to cultivate this crucial capacity, empowering Gen Z to not only survive but thrive by creatively combining their skills to meet the challenges of tomorrow.

The Adaptability Advantage: Thriving, Not Just Surviving

Adaptability is more than just reacting to change; it's about proactively embracing it. It's the agility to evolve alongside a constantly shifting world, learning from each change and using it to your advantage. It's a mindset, a constant willingness to learn, grow, and innovate. In essence, adaptability empowers individuals to remain relevant, continue adding value, and seize

113

opportunities even amidst uncertainty. It's the difference between merely surviving and truly thriving.

The pace of change today is unprecedented. Technological disruptions, evolving workplace dynamics, and global challenges demand more than resilience—they require adaptability. For Gen Z entering the workforce, adaptability is not just a skill, but a survival mechanism, a superpower that can define their career trajectory. This is the era where the most adaptable, not necessarily the strongest or smartest, will flourish. Adaptability allows you to pivot when plans falter, embrace uncertainty with confidence, and transform obstacles into opportunities. It's the mindset that turns challenges into stepping stones, ensuring you stay ahead in a world that never stands still.

Common challenges to becoming more adaptable

- Fixed Mindset
- Fear of Failure
- Comfort Zones
- Lack of Self-Awareness
- Resistance to Change
- Lack of Learning Agility
- Poor Problem-Solving Skills
- Emotional Inflexibility
- Lack of Resources or Support
- Cognitive Rigidity

Cultivating the Growth Mindset: The Foundation of Adaptability

At the heart of adaptability lies the growth mindset, a concept championed by psychologist Carol Dweck. This mindset is grounded in the belief that abilities, intelligence, and skills are not fixed, but rather can be developed through dedication, learning, and perseverance. For Gen Z professionals, this translates to viewing challenges as opportunities for growth, not as insurmountable obstacles. This perspective is crucial for navigating the ever-changing environments of industries undergoing rapid technological evolution.

A growth mindset reframes our relationship with uncertainty. Where others perceive change as a threat, those with a growth mindset see it as an invitation to upskill, innovate, and improve. For example, the introduction of new technologies in the workplace can be viewed not as a threat to job security, but as an exciting opportunity to acquire new skills and enhance capabilities. Embracing change also requires cultivating curiosity—a thirst for knowledge and growth at every career stage. This openness to learning encourages professionals to venture beyond their comfort zones and experiment with new ideas, even if it involves taking calculated risks. Flexibility becomes a core trait, as adaptable individuals recognize that clinging to comfort can hinder the unlocking of their true potential.

The COVID-19 pandemic vividly illustrated the importance of adaptability. The sudden shift to remote work was unprecedented, yet those who adapted quickly, mastering digital collaboration tools and maintaining productivity, thrived, while others struggled. This demonstrates how a proactive attitude and a willingness to learn can be decisive in times of crisis.

Reframing Failure: Learning from Setbacks

Failure is an inherent part of growth, yet in a society often obsessed with curated perfection, particularly through social media, it can feel catastrophic. However, reframing failure as a vital learning experience is crucial for cultivating resilience and adaptability. As Michael Jordan famously stated, 'I've missed more than 9,000 shots in my career. I've lost almost 300 games. 26 times, I've been trusted to take the game-winning shot and missed. I've failed over and over and over again in my life. And that is why I succeed.' This powerful declaration underscores a fundamental truth: failure is not the antithesis of success, but rather an integral component.

When we shift our perspective, viewing failure not as a definitive judgment but as an essential step in the learning process, we unlock our capacity to rebound stronger. By objectively dissecting setbacks, we can extract invaluable lessons applicable to future challenges. This transformative shift empowers individuals to approach their endeavours with a spirit of experimentation and curiosity, rather than a debilitating fear of mistakes.

Celebrating incremental victories is equally vital in reframing failure. Each forward step, regardless of its magnitude, represents a triumph contributing to long-term growth. Practicing self-compassion during setbacks is also paramount for maintaining mental well-being and focusing on the overarching goal—recognizing that success is frequently built upon a bedrock of perseverance through failures.

The narratives of innovators like Thomas Edison and Oprah Winfrey serve as compelling reminders that failure often precedes extraordinary achievement. Both encountered numerous setbacks before realizing their remarkable accomplishments. Their resilience and ability to learn from their errors were pivotal to their success, inspiring others to perceive failure as a stepping stone, not a stumbling block, just as Michael Jordan did throughout his legendary career.

Lifelong Learning: Staying Relevant in the Modern Workplace

In an era defined by rapid technological transformation, staying relevant means committing to lifelong learning. The pace of change is accelerating, with industries being reshaped by AI, automation, and digital innovation. Professionals must continuously upskill to remain competitive and valuable in the workforce.

Lifelong learning is no longer a luxury—it's a necessity. Professionals who maintain their skills through continuous education, whether through formal courses, certifications, or self-directed learning, are better positioned to thrive in a rapidly evolving world. A proactive approach to learning is essential, seeking opportunities to acquire new knowledge both within one's field and in complementary areas.

Numerous avenues exist for staying informed and relevant. Online learning platforms like Coursera, LinkedIn Learning, Udemy and Codecademy offer accessible and flexible options for upskilling. Many companies, recognizing the importance of continuous development, are investing in upskilling programs, ensuring their employees are prepared for the future of work. By developing a personalized learning plan that balances technical expertise with soft skills—such as leadership, communication, and problem-solving—professionals can ensure they remain adaptable and capable of navigating the complexities of modern work environments.

Jared's Lifelong Learning Journey

Jared was a phenomenally successful salesperson known for his ability to close deals through face-to-face interactions. For five years, he relied on his established methods, confident in his ability to build rapport and read body language in person. However, the rapid shift to remote work, driven by a global pandemic, disrupted his established routine. Jared realized that the technological transformation was not just a temporary change but a fundamental shift in his industry.

Recognizing that staying relevant meant committing to lifelong learning, Jared decided to proactively upskill. He understood that his past successes wouldn't guarantee future relevance. He enrolled in online courses on virtual selling techniques, focusing on mastering platforms like Zoom, crafting effective email pitches, and analyzing digital engagement metrics. He also sought out certifications in digital marketing and social media strategy, understanding the importance of leveraging these tools for modern sales.

Jared didn't just focus on technical skills. He understood the importance of complementary soft skills. He participated in virtual workshops on leadership and communication, recognizing that these skills were crucial for building trust and rapport in a virtual environment. He even sought out mentorship from younger colleagues, learning how to effectively leverage social media platforms like LinkedIn to connect with prospects and build his professional network.

Within a few months, Jared had transformed himself into a virtual sales expert. His commitment to continuous education allowed him to not only regain his top-performer status but also become a valuable resource for his team. He developed a personalized learning plan for his colleagues, sharing his newfound knowledge and helping them navigate the complexities of virtual sales. His proactive approach to learning and his willingness to embrace discomfort earned him a leadership role, where he continued to champion the importance of lifelong learning within the organization.

Lifelong learning is not just about acquiring new skills; it's about embracing a mindset of continuous growth and adaptability. Jared's story demonstrates that by committing to continuous education and developing a personalized learning plan that balances technical expertise with soft skills, professionals can not only stay relevant but also thrive in the modern workplace.

Adaptability and Innovation: A Powerful Synergy

Adaptability is not just about reacting to change; it fuels innovation. When we embrace change and uncertainty, we open ourselves to creative problem-solving and unconventional solutions. The ability to think creatively, challenge assumptions, and explore new possibilities is at the core of innovation. In a world of constant evolution, this innovative mindset is critical for staying ahead.

Fostering creativity requires a willingness to question the status quo and collaborate with diverse teams to generate fresh perspectives. This creates an environment where new ideas can flourish, leading to bolder and more forward-thinking solutions. Netflix's evolution from a DVD rental service to a global streaming giant exemplifies how adaptability can drive innovation. Netflix disrupted the entertainment industry by recognizing shifting consumer preferences and leveraging emerging technology. This ability to pivot quickly and seize new opportunities has been crucial to their continued success. For Gen Z, who have grown up in a world of constant technological change, this kind of innovative thinking should come naturally.

Key Components of Adaptability for Gen Z Professionals:

♦ **Agility:** Learning agility involves being curious, seeking out new information, and being open to different perspectives. For Gen Z, this means actively engaging with new technologies, exploring different fields of interest, and being willing to learn from mentors and peers. They should be comfortable with the rapid pace of information flow and be able to quickly synthesize and apply new knowledge.

♦ **Problem Solving:** Strong problem-solving skills enable individuals to adapt their approach and find creative solutions to new challenges. Gen Z professionals should focus on developing their analytical skills, critical thinking, and the ability to approach problems from multiple angles. They should be comfortable with ambiguity and be able to develop solutions even with incomplete information.

♦ **Open-Mindedness:** Open-minded individuals are willing to consider alternative viewpoints and adapt their own beliefs and behaviors accordingly. Gen Z should be open to feedback, willing to challenge their own assumptions, and comfortable working with people from diverse backgrounds. They should be able to appreciate different perspectives and incorporate them into their own thinking.

Flexibility Vs Adaptability

Flexibility is the willingness to adjust plans or approaches to changing circumstances, like offering flexible work hours or shifting priorities. It's about modifying thoughts and behaviors to suit different situations and being open to new options. Adaptability, however, goes deeper. It's the ability to not just change but to *thrive* in new or unfamiliar environments over the long term. It involves learning, growing, and adapting strategies to succeed in unfamiliar territory, even amidst major shifts, like a company changing its entire business model. Essentially, flexibility is about bending with the wind, while adaptability is about growing strong roots even in a storm, allowing you to learn and flourish from experiences outside your comfort zone.

Practical Exercises for Cultivating Adaptability

Developing adaptability requires engaging in activities that challenge our thinking and push us beyond our comfort zones. Practical exercises can help cultivate this skill, allowing individuals to view change as an opportunity for growth rather than a source of fear.

One such exercise is the Mindset Shifting Journal, where individuals document instances of facing change and reflect on their adaptation strategies. This practice reinforces the idea that change is not something to resist, but rather to embrace. Stretch assignments—taking on projects that expand personal boundaries and require new skills or perspectives—are another valuable exercise. Scenario planning exercises, where professionals practice responding to hypothetical disruptions, can prepare them for real-world challenges, such as the introduction of new technology or crisis management.

Thriving in Times of Disruption: Adaptability as a Strategy

In a world that's constantly changing, adaptability is more than just a way to survive – it's the key to thriving. Whether it's dealing with the rise of artificial intelligence, facing global challenges, or navigating economic shifts, those who can adapt have a big advantage. As Charles Darwin wisely said, "It is not the strongest or the smartest that survive, but the ones who can adapt to change."

This idea, originally about evolution, holds true in today's professional world. By embracing change with confidence and flexibility, individuals and organizations can stay agile even when things are uncertain. This agility helps them not only get through tough times but also turn challenges into opportunities for growth and innovation. Those who resist change struggle to keep up, while adaptable people and companies continue to move forward. In essence, adaptability transforms disruption from a threat into a catalyst for advancement, proving that the ability to evolve is the most potent strategy for success in a rapidly changing world.

Maya, The Catalyst for Change

Maya was a dedicated high school science teacher, passionate about sparking curiosity in her students. However, she felt increasingly limited by traditional teaching methods. When the school abruptly shifted to online learning due to an unforeseen global health crisis, many of her colleagues were overwhelmed and struggled to maintain student engagement. Maya, however, saw this disruption as a unique opportunity to innovate.

Instead of lamenting the loss of in-person interaction, Maya embraced the challenge with confidence. Recognizing that adaptability was her key to success, she immersed herself in the world of digital learning. With no prior tech expertise, she spent countless hours exploring virtual labs, gamified learning platforms, and augmented reality applications. She even took free online coding courses, determined to create interactive and engaging lesson plans tailored to the virtual environment.

One of her most successful innovations was a collaborative virtual ecosystem project. Students worked in teams to design and manage virtual habitats, solving complex scientific problems to ensure their ecosystem's survival. This project not only boosted student engagement but also fostered critical thinking and problem-solving skills. Word of Maya's innovative teaching spread, and her methods were soon adopted district-wide, transforming the way science was taught online.

Seeing the potential for wider impact, Maya launched an educational technology startup. She developed a platform that provided educators with access to a library of interactive virtual learning resources, empowering them to adapt to the ever-evolving landscape of education. She credited her adaptability for not only surviving the disruption but for thriving, transforming a crisis into a catalyst for positive change. She had demonstrated that adaptability isn't just a reaction to change; it's a powerful strategy for innovation and growth.

In a world of constant evolution, adaptability is the superpower that unlocks potential and keeps professionals ahead of the curve. By embracing change, cultivating a growth mindset, reframing failure, committing to lifelong learning, and fostering innovation, Gen Z professionals can not only survive but truly thrive in the modern workplace. They are the generation poised to decode the future, not just survive it. By honing their adaptability superpower, they can shape the future and make it their own.

Actionable Exercises:

1. **Change Challenge:** For one week, pick a routine or habit in your daily life and change it. This could be your work schedule, how you communicate, or how you solve problems. After the week, think about how this change affected your productivity, creativity, and flexibility.

2. **Growth Mindset Reflection:** Take 10 minutes to think about a recent change or challenge you faced. Write down what the change was, how you initially reacted, what you learned, and

how you adapted. Review your notes and think about how you can use this mindset in future situations.

3. **Scenario Planning Exercise:** Imagine a potential change in your career or industry that could happen in the next 6 months. Think of three possible scenarios: the best-case, the worst-case, and the most likely. For each scenario, create an action plan to help you stay adaptable.

4. **Flexibility Stretch:** For one week, intentionally say "yes" to opportunities or tasks outside your usual responsibilities, like helping a colleague or taking on a different type of work. After the week, think about how adapting to these new situations felt and what you learned.

5. **Feedback Loop:** Ask a colleague or mentor for feedback on how adaptable you've been in recent projects or situations. Specifically, ask how you handled unexpected changes and how you can improve your adaptability in the future.

Key Takeaways:

1. **Adaptability is Essential:** In a rapidly changing world, adaptability is a crucial skill for thriving, not just surviving.

2. **Growth Mindset is Key:** Believing that abilities can be developed through dedication and learning is foundational to adaptability.

3. **Failure is a Learning Opportunity:** Reframing failure as a valuable learning experience builds resilience and adaptability.

4. **Lifelong Learning is Necessary:** Continuously upskilling and seeking new knowledge is essential for staying relevant in the modern workplace.

5. **Adaptability Fuels Innovation:** Embracing change and uncertainty opens the door to creative problem-solving and innovation.

6. **Agility is Crucial:** Being curious, seeking new information, and being open to different perspectives are important aspects of learning agility.

7. **Problem-Solving Skills are Vital:** Strong problem-solving skills enable individuals to adapt their approach and find creative solutions.

8. **Open-Mindedness is Important:** Being willing to consider alternative viewpoints and adapt beliefs and behaviors is key.

9. **Flexibility and Adaptability Differ:** Flexibility is about adjusting plans, while adaptability is about thriving in new environments long-term.

10. **Adaptability is a Strategy:** It's not just a reaction to change; it's a proactive approach to turning challenges into opportunities.

Chapter 8

TIME MANAGEMENT FOR THE DISTRACTED GENERATION: PRIORITIZE LIKE A PRO

In today's digital age, where distractions are abundant and the pressure to do more is ever-present, mastering time management is no longer just a valuable skill—it's a superpower. For Gen Z, the first generation to grow up fully immersed in the digital world, the challenge is even greater. But amidst the noise and chaos lies an opportunity: to reclaim your time, boost your productivity, and design a life that is both successful and fulfilling.

This comprehensive guide will equip you with the knowledge and tools to navigate the complexities of the modern world and prioritize like a pro. We'll explore time-tested principles and cutting-edge techniques, all tailored to the unique needs and challenges of Gen Z. Let's dive in and turn time management from a challenge into your greatest strength.

Mastering Prioritization: The Eisenhower Matrix

In a world of competing priorities, it's easy to feel overwhelmed and scattered. The Eisenhower Matrix, also known as the Urgent-Important Matrix, offers a simple yet powerful framework for prioritizing tasks and making decisions. This matrix categorizes tasks into four quadrants:

1. **Do First:** Tasks that are both urgent and important (e.g., deadlines, crises).

2. **Decide When:** Tasks that are important but not urgent (e.g., long-term goals, planning, relationship building).

3. **Delegate:** Tasks that are urgent but not important (e.g., interruptions, some meetings, other people's minor issues).

4. **Delete:** Tasks that are neither urgent nor important (e.g., time-wasting activities, distractions).

By using this matrix, you can quickly identify which tasks deserve your immediate attention and which can be delegated, deferred, or eliminated altogether. This allows you to focus your time and energy on activities that truly matter and contribute to your long-term goals.

Overcoming Digital Overload: Focus in a Distracted World

The digital age has brought incredible tools and opportunities, but it has also created a constant barrage of distractions. From social media notifications to the endless stream of information available online, it's easy to get sidetracked and lose focus.

To overcome digital overload, you need to develop digital hygiene habits. This involves setting boundaries and creating systems to manage your digital environment. Some effective strategies include:

- Scheduling specific times to check emails and social media.

- Turning off non-essential notifications.

- Using website blockers to avoid time-wasting websites.

- Decluttering your digital workspace (e.g., organizing your inbox, unsubscribing from unnecessary emails).

- Creating "focus zones" in your physical environment, free from distractions.

By implementing these strategies, you can reclaim your attention and create space for deep, focused work.

The Power of the "One Big Thing"

Emma, a Gen Z entrepreneur, ran a thriving online jewellery business but constantly felt overwhelmed by endless notifications, emails, and competing demands. Each morning, she started with ambitious plans, but by the end of the day, she often found herself frustrated, wondering where the time had gone.

One day, a mentor introduced her to the concept of the "One Big Thing" (OBT)—choosing the single most important task each day that would drive the greatest impact. Instead of reacting to every distraction, Emma decided to put this into practice. Each morning, she wrote her OBT on a sticky note and placed it on her laptop—a constant reminder to focus.

At first, resisting the urge to multitask was difficult. She often caught herself reaching for her phone or checking emails out of habit. But as she stuck to her OBT routine, she noticed a shift. When she dedicated two uninterrupted hours to designing a new product line, she saw a 20% increase in sales—a far greater impact than the hours she previously spent responding to messages.

Over time, Emma's productivity soared, and her stress levels dropped. She realized that focusing on one high-impact task each day helped her make consistent progress toward her goals, rather than feeling trapped in an endless cycle of busywork.

Time management for the distracted generation starts with clarity—focusing on one high-impact task each day can break the cycle of overwhelm and boost productivity.

Building Productive Habits That Stick

Time management isn't a one-time effort; it's about creating habits that sustain productivity over the long term. Habits are the building blocks of consistency, and the science of habit formation emphasizes the power of small, incremental changes.

For Gen Z, habit-stacking—attaching a new habit to an existing one—can be particularly effective. For instance, you could review your daily priorities while enjoying your morning coffee or set a "wind-down" alarm to signal the end of screen time.

Other productive habits include:

- Daily reflection and planning: Taking a few minutes each day to review your progress, identify areas for improvement, and plan for the day ahead.

- Time blocking: Scheduling specific blocks of time for different activities, such as focused work, creative pursuits, and breaks.

- Regularly reviewing and updating your goals: Ensuring that your daily actions are aligned with your long-term vision.

By incorporating these habits into your routine, you can create a sustainable system for productivity and achieve your goals with greater ease and consistency.

The Role of Technology in Productivity

Technology, when used mindfully, can be a powerful ally in your productivity journey. There's a wide range of tools and apps designed to help you manage your time, organize tasks, and minimize distractions.

Some popular options include:

- Project management tools: Asana, Trello, Monday.com
- Focus apps: Forest, Freedom, Cold Turkey

- Note-taking apps: Evernote, Notion, Google Keep

- Calendar apps: Google Calendar, Fantastical, Outlook Calendar

Experiment with different tools to find what works best for you and integrate them into your workflow to streamline your efforts and boost your efficiency.

Resilience in Time Management

Even with the best strategies in place, setbacks are inevitable. Deadlines may be missed, schedules disrupted, or priorities reshuffled. That's where resilience comes in.

Resilience is the ability to bounce back from challenges and adapt to changing circumstances. It's about viewing setbacks as learning opportunities and using them to refine your strategies and improve your approach.

To cultivate resilience in your time management practices:

- Reframe failure as feedback: Instead of dwelling on mistakes, analyze what went wrong and identify areas for improvement.

- Practice self-compassion: Be kind to yourself when things don't go as planned. Remember that everyone makes mistakes, and it's okay to adjust your course as needed.

- Seek support from others: Talk to mentors, friends, or colleagues for guidance and encouragement.

- Celebrate your successes: Acknowledge your accomplishments and use them as motivation to keep moving forward.

By developing resilience, you can navigate the inevitable ups and downs of life with greater ease and confidence, ensuring that you stay on track toward your goals even when faced with challenges.

Deep Work: Your Secret Weapon in a Distracted World

In a world where attention is a scarce commodity, deep work is your superpower. Coined by Georgetown professor Cal Newport, deep work is the ability to focus without distraction on a cognitively demanding task. It's about cultivating a state of flow where you're fully immersed in your work and producing your best results.

To integrate deep work into your routine:

- **Schedule dedicated blocks of time for deep work:** Treat these blocks as sacred appointments and protect them from interruptions.

- **Create a distraction-free environment:** Find a quiet workspace, turn off notifications, and communicate your availability to others.

- **Start small and gradually increase your deep work sessions:** Begin with 15-20 minutes of focused work and gradually increase the duration as you build your concentration muscles.

- **Take breaks strategically:** Short breaks can help you recharge and return to your work with renewed focus.

By mastering the art of deep work, you can unlock your cognitive potential, achieve extraordinary results, and stand out from the crowd in an increasingly competitive world.

The 90-Minute Focus Rule

Arjun, a marketing intern at a global media company, constantly struggled to meet deadlines. Despite working long hours, his productivity suffered due to constant distractions—Slack messages, social media pings, and an endless stream of meetings. His workdays felt chaotic, and the breaking point came when he missed a critical project deadline. Concerned, his manager stepped in.

Instead of reprimanding him, his manager introduced him to the "90-Minute Focus Rule." He explained that the human brain operates in 90-minute cycles of peak concentration, followed by short recovery periods. Arjun decided to put this into practice.

He began blocking uninterrupted 90-minute sessions in his calendar for deep work, treating them as non-negotiable appointments. He silenced notifications, placed his phone in another room, and closed unnecessary browser tabs. During these focus blocks, he tackled high-priority tasks like crafting marketing strategies and designing presentations. He then scheduled meetings and administrative tasks during his lower-energy periods.

The impact was immediate. Arjun found that he accomplished in 90 minutes what previously took him half a day. His efficiency soared, and his work quality improved. More importantly, he no longer felt drained by the end of the day. By aligning his schedule with his brain's natural rhythm, he transformed his work habits—delivering projects ahead of deadlines and gaining recognition from his team.

Time management isn't just about working harder—it's about working smarter by aligning your efforts with your brain's natural focus cycles.

Hyperfocus and Scatterfocus: The Dynamic Duo of Productivity

Your attention is a versatile tool that can be used in different ways depending on the task at hand. Hyperfocus is like a laser beam, allowing you to concentrate intensely on a single task and achieve peak performance. Scatterfocus, on the other hand, is like a floodlight, allowing your mind to wander and make connections between seemingly disparate ideas.

Both hyperfocus and scatterfocus are essential for productivity and creativity. Hyperfocus allows you to tackle complex tasks and produce high-quality work, while scatterfocus enables you to generate new ideas, solve problems creatively, and gain fresh perspectives.

To harness the power of both:

- **Be intentional about when you use each mode:** Engage hyperfocus for tasks that require deep concentration and scatterfocus for brainstorming, reflection, and creative exploration.

- **Create environments that support each mode:** A quiet workspace with minimal distractions is ideal for hyperfocus, while a stimulating environment with access to diverse information sources can facilitate scatterfocus.

- **Practice switching between modes:** Learn to transition smoothly between hyperfocus and scatterfocus as needed throughout your day.

By understanding and utilizing both modes of attention, you can optimize your productivity, tap into your creative potential, and achieve a greater sense of balance and fulfillment in your work.

Chaya, the Content Creator

Chaya is a popular content creator on YouTube and LinkedIn. She specializes in educational videos about sustainable living. Her work requires a blend of creativity, research, and meticulous execution.

Hyperfocus in Action:

When Chaya is editing a complex video, she enters a state of hyperfocus. She sets her phone to "Do Not Disturb," closes all unnecessary tabs, and puts on noise-canceling headphones. Her workspace is clean and organized, minimizing distractions. During these hyperfocus sessions, she meticulously reviews footage, fine-tunes audio, and adds graphics. She's deeply immersed in the task, allowing her to produce high-quality, polished videos. Also when she is researching a complicated topic, like the effects of micro plastics in the ocean, she uses hyperfocus to read scientific articles, and to take detailed notes.

Scatterfocus in Action:

Chaya understands that creativity doesn't always come from staring at a screen. She often takes "scatterfocus walks" in nature, allowing her mind to wander. During these walks, she might listen to a podcast, observe her surroundings, or simply daydream. These scatterfocus sessions are where she generates new video ideas, connects seemingly unrelated concepts, and finds creative solutions to problems. She might see a discarded plastic bottle and suddenly envision a video about upcycling. She also uses scatterfocus while scrolling through her social media feeds. She is not looking for anything specific, but she is looking for trends, news, and new ideas that she can use in her content.

Switching Between Modes:

Chaya has learned to intentionally schedule her day to balance hyperfocus and scatterfocus. She might spend the morning editing videos (hyperfocus) and the afternoon brainstorming new content (scatterfocus). She uses techniques like the Pomodoro Technique to transition between modes. After a hyperfocus session, she takes a short break to stretch or listen to music, allowing her mind to reset before engaging in scatterfocus. She has also learned that if she is having trouble getting into a hyperfocus state, that a short scatterfocus activity, like a walk around the block, can help her to clear her mind, and then return to the task refreshed. It shows how both focus types help in real work.

Make Time: Designing Your Day, Not Just Surviving It

Traditional time management often focuses on efficiency and squeezing as much as possible into your day. Make Time, a framework developed by Jake Knapp and John Zeratsky, offers a different approach. It's about being intentional with your time, prioritizing what truly matters, and designing your day around those priorities.

The core principles of Make Time are:

♦ **Highlight:** Identify the one activity that you want to prioritize each day. This is the task that will bring you the most satisfaction or move you closer to your goals.

♦ **Laser:** Protect your "Laser Time"—the dedicated time for your Highlight—by minimizing distractions and creating a focused environment.

♦ **Energize:** Take care of your physical and mental well-being by getting enough sleep, exercising regularly, and engaging in activities that bring you joy.

♦ **Reflect:** Review your day and identify what worked well and what could be improved. Use this feedback to refine your approach and make time work for you, not against you.

By implementing these principles, you can shift from a reactive to a proactive approach to time management, ensuring that you're spending your time on activities that align with your values and contribute to your overall well-being.

Beyond the 9-to-5 Grind: Charting Your Own Course

Gen Z is challenging the traditional 9-to-5 grind and seeking alternative paths that offer greater flexibility, purpose, and fulfillment. Whether it's starting a side hustle, freelancing, or building a business, Gen Z is embracing entrepreneurship and innovation to create careers that fit their lifestyles and values.

To chart your own course:

♦ **Identify your passions and skills:** What are you good at? What do you enjoy doing?

- **Explore different career options:** Research various industries and roles to find what aligns with your interests and goals.

- **Develop your skills and knowledge:** Invest in your education and acquire the skills needed to succeed in your chosen field.

- **Network with like-minded individuals:** Connect with people who inspire you, support you, and challenge you to grow.

- **Embrace challenges and learn from your mistakes:** Failure is a natural part of the learning process. Use setbacks as opportunities to grow and improve.

By taking ownership of your career path and embracing a growth mindset, you can create a fulfilling and successful career that aligns with your passions and values.

Hacking Your Productivity: Gen Z Edition

Here are some additional tips tailored to the Gen Z experience:

- **Explore online courses:** Unlock new skills and knowledge by enrolling in online courses tailored to your interests and expertise. Whether you're advancing in your current job or pursuing a new passion, there are courses for almost everything. Many are flexible, allowing you to learn at your own pace, and some offer live sessions with expert instructors. Online learning can help boost your skills and open up new opportunities.

- **Build your network:** Connect with like-minded individuals online and offline. Attend industry events, join online communities, and build meaningful relationships.

- **Learn to say no:** Protect your time and energy by saying no to commitments that don't align with your priorities.

- **Prioritize your well-being:** Don't burn out. Make time for exercise, mindfulness, and activities that bring you joy.

- **Embrace lifelong learning:** The world is changing rapidly. Stay curious, keep learning new skills, and adapt to the evolving landscape.

- **Find your tribe:** Surround yourself with people who inspire you, support you, and challenge you to grow.

- **Don't be afraid to fail:** Failure is a learning opportunity. Embrace setbacks, learn from your mistakes, and keep moving forward.

- **Master your tech:** Don't let your devices control you. Customize your notifications, use focus modes, and schedule "digital detox" periods.

- **Design your ideal lifestyle:** What does your dream life look like? Define your goals, create a plan, and take action.

The Sharp Axe of Time

Once upon a time, in a small village, there was a young man named Aric, known for his incredible strength but frustrated by his inability to find meaningful work. One day, he heard of a wood-cutting job in a nearby forest and eagerly rushed to meet the forest master, Thorne. Impressed by his strength, Thorne agrees to hire him.

"Strength is important," Thorne said, "but remember, it's not just about working hard—it's about working smart."

Aric, confident in his abilities, didn't fully listen. He grabbed his axe and set to work, swinging it with all his might to cut as many trees as possible. For hours, he worked tirelessly, but by midday, his arms ached, and his progress slowed significantly.

Seeing this, Thorne approached him and said, "Aric, you're strong, but your axe is dull. If you take time to sharpen it, you'll cut more trees with less effort."

Although Aric was hesitant, he paused and sharpened his axe as Thorne suggested. When he returned to work, he was amazed at the difference. His swings became smoother, and trees fell faster with far less effort.

Over time, Aric learned the true power of working smarter, not just harder. He began to prioritize sharpening his tools and pacing himself. This approach not only made him more efficient but also kept him from becoming overly exhausted. Soon, Aric became the village's most sought-after craftsman, admired not just for his strength but for his wisdom and strategic approach to work.

Aric's story holds an important lesson for today's fast-paced world, where people often feel pressured to do more and more. As Abraham Lincoln famously said, "Give me six hours to chop down a tree and I will spend the first four sharpening the axe."

This quote perfectly embodies the idea that success doesn't come from frantic multitasking or endless effort. Like sharpening an axe, time management is about preparation, focus, and working with purpose. It's about aligning your tasks with your energy, taking breaks to recharge, and using your tools—or your time— wisely. In the end, true success comes not from relentless effort, but from thoughtful, efficient actions. The sharpest axe, after all, cuts through the toughest wood with the least amount of force.

The Future is Yours to Create

Gen Z possesses the unique capacity to redefine the landscape of work and life. Your inherent tech fluency, creative drive, and passion for impact are powerful assets. By cultivating focused attention, embracing intentional productivity, and designing lives of purpose, you can forge a future that is both successful and deeply fulfilling. It's time to break free from distractions, unleash your potential, and create a world where work and life seamlessly integrate, forming a cohesive whole—a design you control.

As Stephen Covey wisely stated, 'The key is not to prioritize what's on your schedule, but to schedule your priorities.' This principle is paramount for Gen Z. Time management isn't about maximizing output; it's about strategically allocating your most precious resource—time—to what truly matters. By prioritizing your core goals, establishing productive habits, and leveraging technology mindfully, you can reclaim your time, achieve your aspirations, and live a life aligned with your purpose. Ultimately, the power to shape your future resides within your hands.

Effective Time Management Tools and Techniques:

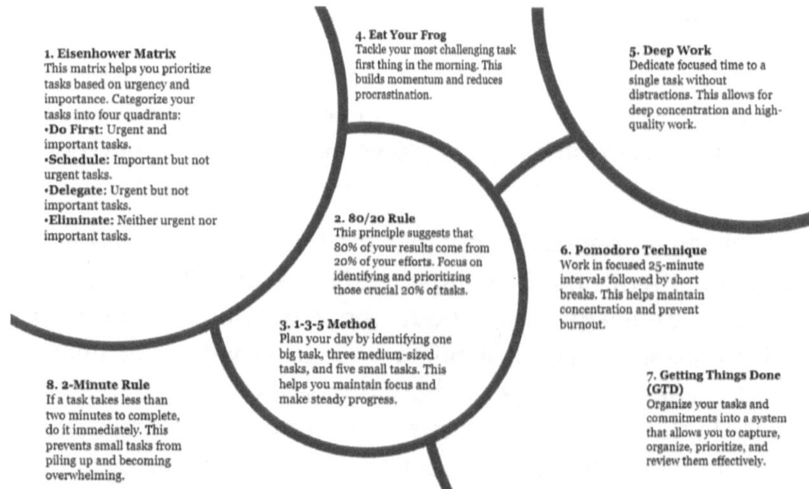

Actionable Exercises:

1. **Prioritize Your Day with the Eisenhower Matrix:** Draw a grid with four sections: Urgent and Important, Not Urgent but Important, Urgent but Not Important, and Not Urgent and Not Important. At the start of each day, write down all your tasks and put them in the right section. Focus on the "Urgent and Important" and "Not Urgent but Important" tasks first.

2. **Time-Blocking Exercise:** Pick a task or project you need to finish and break it into smaller steps. Use time-blocking to set aside specific hours in your day to work on each step without any interruptions. For example, set aside one hour in the

morning for research and another hour for writing. Stick to your schedule and get rid of distractions during those times.

3. **The 2-Minute Rule:** If a task will take you 2 minutes or less, do it right away. This will stop small tasks from piling up and making you feel overwhelmed. Keep track of how many times you use this rule in a week and see how much it helps your productivity.

4. **Set a Weekly Review:** At the end of each week, spend 15-20 minutes looking back on your progress. Ask yourself what tasks you prioritized well, what distractions got in your way, and what you accomplished. Use this time to change your priorities for the next week and make sure you're focusing on what's important.

5. **Eliminate Digital Distractions:** Find the apps or websites that distract you the most. Use apps like Forest or Focus@Will to stay focused, or set your phone to "Do Not Disturb" during work times. Think about using browser extensions to block distracting websites during work hours. Track your progress and see how much more focused you become.

Key Takeaways:

1. **Master Prioritization:** Use tools like the Eisenhower Matrix to focus on tasks that truly matter.

2. **Combat Digital Overload:** Set boundaries and use digital hygiene habits to minimize distractions.

3. **Focus on "One Big Thing":** Choose one high-impact task each day to drive the greatest progress.

4. **Build Productive Habits:** Use habit-stacking and time-blocking to create a sustainable system for productivity.

5. **Use Technology Wisely:** Leverage productivity tools to manage time and organize tasks effectively.

6. **Cultivate Resilience:** Reframe setbacks as learning opportunities and practice self-compassion.

7. **Practice Deep Work:** Schedule dedicated blocks of time for focused work to achieve peak performance.

8. **Understand Your Attention:** Use both hyperfocus and scatterfocus to optimize productivity and creativity.

9. **Design Your Day Intentionally:** Prioritize what truly matters and align your time with your values.

10. **Embrace Lifelong Learning:** Continuously develop skills and adapt to the evolving landscape of work and life.

Chapter 9

RESILIENCE REDEFINED: NAVIGATING SETBACKS IN A FAST-PACED WORLD

In today's fast-paced world, resilience is no longer just a nice-to-have trait; it's a must-have, especially for Gen Z. With constant pressure from instant gratification, nonstop social media, and a changing economy, the ability to bounce back is key. Resilience isn't about avoiding failures; it's about recovering from them. As Ralph Waldo Emerson said, "Our greatest glory is not in never failing, but in rising up every time we fail." This quote captures the heart of resilience—turning setbacks into opportunities to grow. This chapter explores the multifaceted nature of resilience, offering actionable strategies to transform setbacks into springboards for growth, cultivate mental well-being, and build a robust foundation for personal and professional success.

Reframing Failure: From Stigma to Stepping Stone

For too long, failure has been stigmatized as a mark of inadequacy. However, a shift in perspective, championed by psychologist Carol Dweck's growth mindset, reframes failure as an invaluable learning opportunity. This mindset emphasizes that abilities and intelligence are not fixed but can be developed through dedication and effort. This is particularly crucial for Gen Z, who face the amplified pressures of curated social media lives, often exacerbating the fear of falling short.

Reframing failure requires a conscious effort to rewrite our internal narrative. Instead of viewing setbacks as personal failings, we must see them as data points on our journey. A failed project, for instance, can illuminate areas for skill development or highlight more effective collaboration strategies. The stories of successful individuals like J.K. Rowling, who faced numerous rejections before achieving literary stardom, serve as powerful reminders that failure is often a precursor to success. By embracing this perspective, we transform failure from a source of shame into a catalyst for growth.

Cultivating Mental Fitness: Strength from Within

In our high-pressure world, mental fitness is just as important as physical fitness. It's not about eliminating stress altogether but rather developing the skills to manage it effectively. Practices like mindfulness, meditation, and reflective journaling empower us to stay grounded and present amidst the chaos.

Mindfulness cultivates a non-judgmental awareness of the present moment. It can be as simple as taking a few deep breaths during a stressful situation or practicing gratitude to shift our focus from negativity to abundance. Journaling provides a safe space to process emotions, identify recurring patterns, and gain clarity, fostering emotional resilience over time.

Burnout, a significant challenge for Gen Z, requires proactive management. Recognizing the early warning signs—emotional exhaustion, declining performance, cynicism—is crucial. Prioritizing self-care, whether it's taking breaks, pursuing hobbies, or seeking professional support, is essential for maintaining mental fitness. By making self-care a non-negotiable part of our lives, we build the reserves needed to weather life's storms.

Gratitude and Reflection: Anchors for Resilience

Gratitude, a seemingly simple practice, has profound effects on our well-being. By consciously focusing on the positive aspects of our lives, even during challenging times, we shift our perspective and build emotional strength. Research consistently demonstrates that gratitude enhances mental health, strengthens relationships, and increases overall life satisfaction.

Reflection complements gratitude by fostering self-awareness. Regularly evaluating our experiences, celebrating our progress, and extracting lessons from our setbacks keeps us grounded and resilient. A simple reflective practice, like writing down three things that went well each day, can create a positive feedback loop, nurturing optimism and reinforcing a growth mindset.

The Power of Support Systems: Strength in Connection

Resilience is rarely built in isolation. Strong support systems—mentors, peers, communities—provide encouragement, perspective, and practical assistance during challenging times.

Mentors offer invaluable guidance, sharing their wisdom and experiences to help us navigate difficult situations. Their insights can provide context and direction, helping us see the bigger picture. Peers offer empathy and shared understanding, particularly when facing similar challenges. Communities, whether professional networks or personal circles, foster a sense of belonging and remind us that we are not alone. Highlighting the stories of individuals who attribute their success to supportive relationships underscores the transformative power of human connection. Actively seeking mentorship, nurturing friendships, and engaging in communities are crucial steps in building a resilience toolkit.

Mental Agility: Thriving in Uncertainty

In an era defined by rapid technological advancements and constant disruption, mental agility—the ability to adapt and pivot—is a cornerstone of resilience. It allows us to respond flexibly to challenges, seize emerging opportunities, and maintain optimism in the face of uncertainty.

Developing mental agility begins with embracing change as a constant. Instead of resisting the unknown, we can focus on what we *can* control and approach new situations with curiosity. Techniques like scenario planning, which involves anticipating various outcomes and developing adaptable strategies, can boost our confidence and preparedness. Cultivating optimism, another key component, encourages us to view obstacles as opportunities for growth. A missed promotion, for example, can be reframed as a chance to develop new skills or explore alternative career paths.

Self-Care: The Foundation of Resilience

Resilience is deeply rooted in self-care. Prioritizing our physical, mental, and emotional well-being ensures we have the capacity to navigate life's challenges. Self-care is not indulgent; it's essential. For Gen Z, who often juggle career ambitions with societal expectations, prioritizing self-care is a radical act of self-preservation.

Physical health—regular exercise, balanced nutrition, sufficient sleep—is a critical component. These habits enhance energy levels, improve focus, and reduce stress. Emotional self-care involves setting boundaries, saying no to overcommitment, and making time for personal interests. Nurturing passions and engaging in activities that bring joy—painting, hiking, playing music—recharges our resilience reserves, enabling us to face challenges with renewed vigour.

Grit: Passion and Perseverance

Success isn't solely determined by talent; it's shaped by grit—the unwavering determination to persevere despite obstacles. Grit emphasizes the importance of passion and perseverance in achieving long-term goals, especially when faced with setbacks. It's not an innate trait, but a quality that can be cultivated through consistent effort and a deep commitment to our purpose. Passion fuels the journey, while perseverance keeps us moving forward, even when the path gets tough.

The Grit Scale, a research-based questionnaire, measures perseverance and passion, revealing that grit, rather than talent alone, is a strong predictor of success. Studies across various fields, from education and sports to business and the military, demonstrate that individuals with higher levels of grit often outperform their more naturally talented peers who lack persistence.

Grit is built on two fundamental pillars: passion and perseverance. Passion goes beyond initial excitement; it's the enduring interest that sustains us through long-term efforts. Perseverance involves sticking to our goals despite obstacles, maintaining effort even when the journey becomes arduous. These elements combine to form the bedrock of grit.

While talent can provide a head start, it's grit that ultimately determines our trajectory. Talent might help us get noticed, but consistent effort ensures growth and achievement. Those who persist through difficulties, like Thomas Edison with his countless attempts to invent the lightbulb, often surpass those with more innate talent who give up prematurely.

Effort is doubly impactful: it develops skill and fuels achievement. Talent may initiate the journey, but effort leads to mastery. And it's through this accumulated skill that significant achievements unfold. Without effort, talent remains untapped potential, while sustained effort leads to extraordinary accomplishments. Failure is not a signal to quit; it's an integral part of the growth process. Setbacks provide invaluable lessons and often pave the way for breakthroughs. Embracing failure, rather than fearing it, is essential for building resilience and continuing the journey towards success.

A growth mindset is crucial for developing grit. When we believe our abilities can be developed through challenging work, we are more likely to persist in the face of challenges. This mindset transforms obstacles into opportunities for growth. Conversely, a fixed mindset—believing that abilities are static—often leads to frustration and discouragement when faced with setbacks. A strong sense of purpose amplifies grit. When we have a clear understanding of *why* we are working towards a goal, we are more likely to persevere, especially during tough times. Support systems—mentors, family, friends—provide encouragement and guidance, helping us maintain focus and motivation.

The Startup That Rose from the Ashes - A Grit-Powered Revival

Sofia, driven by a deep passion to revolutionize personal finance, co-founded a tech startup. For two years, she and her team poured their hearts and significant funding into developing an innovative app. However, the launch was a crushing blow. The app's complex interface alienated users, resulting in an 80% user base decline within six months. Investors, seeing the failure, began to withdraw, leaving Sofia feeling utterly defeated.

The initial shock was immense. Sofia faced waves of self-doubt, questioning her abilities and the entire venture. However, deep within, her perseverance began to stir. Instead of succumbing to despair, she remembered her initial purpose: to empower people with financial control. She understood that failure was not a signal to quit, but an opportunity to learn and grow.

Sofia gathered her team, fostering a growth mindset by asking, "What did we learn, and how can we rebuild?" They embraced the harsh feedback, conducting extensive user interviews. The team realized they had prioritized flashy features over user experience, neglecting the core need for simplicity.

Sofia, fuelled by her enduring passion, led a pivotal shift. They decided to focus on a single, core function: effortless expense tracking. The team worked tirelessly, demonstrating unwavering perseverance despite the lack of guarantees. They embraced the long hours and challenges, viewing each obstacle as a chance to refine their skills and deepen their understanding. This effort, doubly impactful, started to develop their skill and fuelled their achievement.

Sofia's grit was evident in her unwavering commitment to the goal, even when the path was arduous. She cultivated a strong sense of purpose, reminding herself and her team why they had started this journey. They had a clear understanding of why they were working towards their goal, and this helped them persevere.

The relaunch, born from their hard-earned lessons and relentless perseverance, was a resounding success. Within a year, the simplified app became a top-rated tool, regaining users and attracting new investors. Sofia's startup didn't just bounce back; it rose from the ashes stronger, proving that grit, not just talent, determined their trajectory.

Resilience, powered by grit, is about embracing setbacks as stepping stones. It's about combining passion with perseverance, cultivating a growth mindset, and understanding that effort, guided by purpose, leads to mastery and extraordinary accomplishments.

The Stoic Approach: Turning Adversity into Strength

Stoic philosophy offers powerful tools for navigating life's challenges. The Stoic approach can be summarized in three stages: Perception, Action, and Will. By adjusting our perception, we can view obstacles as opportunities for growth rather than threats. We then take action—often small but deliberate steps—that propel us forward. Finally, willpower—our internal strength to endure and persist—enables us to push through when progress seems slow.

Our perception of challenges often dictates whether we overcome them or succumb to them. Shifting our perspective can reveal new solutions and insights. The way we choose to react to external circumstances is a powerful tool for personal growth. While we cannot control external events, we can always control our responses. Small, consistent actions can lead to significant progress. Resilience is not a sprint; it's a marathon. The challenges we face may not be resolved overnight, but with patience and persistent effort, they can become stepping stones to greater achievements. Over time, adversity can build strength and character.

Bouncing Forward: Resilience Beyond Recovery

True resilience is more than simply bouncing back to our previous state. It's about bouncing *forward*, embracing change, and discovering new growth opportunities. This approach emphasizes evolving through hardship, not just returning to a baseline. People who find meaning in their suffering often experience post-traumatic growth, emerging from tragedy stronger, wiser, and more capable.

While resilience is an individual trait, it thrives in a supportive environment. A strong network of friends, family, or colleagues is essential during tough times. Social connections ease the emotional burden of hardship and provide crucial encouragement. Practicing self-compassion is equally vital. It's not about suppressing emotions but acknowledging them—recognizing that it's okay to grieve while still moving forward. Finding purpose in adversity is another powerful aspect of bouncing forward. Grief and hardship can lead to a re-evaluation of priorities, opening up new paths for growth. By embracing change, individuals can discover new passions, redefine their goals, and emerge stronger than before. Effective leadership is crucial in times of difficulty. Leaders who demonstrate empathy and create supportive environments empower their teams to thrive even in adversity. By fostering an atmosphere of understanding and flexibility, organizations can help individuals navigate personal challenges and build resilience, ensuring collective progress.

Liam: From Shattered Dreams to Transformative Purpose

At 19, Liam was a promising track and field athlete, his sights set on the national team. However, a devastating Achilles tendon tear during a pivotal race abruptly ended his athletic career.

The injury plunged Liam into a profound period of grief. He wasn't just losing a sport; he was losing a part of himself. He struggled with his identity, questioning his purpose without his athletic aspirations. This period was marked by intense emotional pain, and Liam had to learn to practice self-compassion, acknowledging his grief rather than suppressing it. He allowed himself to grieve, understanding it was a natural part of his journey.

One day, his coach offered a transformative piece of advice: "You may not run again, but your discipline and determination can take you anywhere." This sparked a shift in Liam's perspective. He began to explore how his skills and experiences could be channelled into new avenues. He started volunteering as a coach for younger athletes, finding joy in helping them develop their potential. This experience helped him find meaning in his suffering, realizing that his own struggles could empower others.

Liam understood that true resilience was about bouncing forward, not just returning to his previous state. He realized he could evolve through this hardship. Inspired by his own journey, he founded a nonprofit organization dedicated to providing financial and emotional support to injured athletes transitioning out of sports. This initiative allowed him to redefine his goals and discover a new passion.

Through this process, Liam experienced post-traumatic growth. He emerged from his personal tragedy stronger, wiser, and more capable. He embraced the change, allowing his setback to open new paths for growth. His organization thrived, impacting thousands of lives, and he became a renowned speaker on resilience, sharing his story and inspiring others.

Liam's journey exemplified that resilience is about finding new meaning and purpose when life forces you to change course. He didn't just recover; he transformed his setback into a source of strength and purpose for others, demonstrating that true victory lies in the ability to evolve and thrive through adversity. He built a strong network through his nonprofit and through the people he coached, which gave him a strong support system.

Resilience is about bouncing forward, not just back. It involves embracing change, finding meaning in adversity, practicing self-compassion, and evolving into a stronger, more purposeful version of yourself.

Resilience and Reinvention: Navigating the Twists and Turns of Your Career

Gen Z is entering a vastly different professional landscape than previous generations. The traditional career ladder has been replaced by a more dynamic and unpredictable "jungle gym" full of challenges and opportunities. In this environment, resilience isn't just an asset—it's essential for survival and success. Stories of grit and perseverance, from individuals overcoming unimaginable hardship to those breaking barriers through sheer determination, offer valuable lessons for navigating the complexities of modern work.

1. **Finding Your "Why":** The Power of Purpose

   Gen Z seeks purpose in their work, wanting their contributions to have a meaningful impact. This desire isn't a fleeting trend; it's a fundamental human need. Passion fuels our efforts, making challenges less daunting and setbacks less devastating. Finding your "why" is a journey of self-discovery. It involves exploring your skills and talents, identifying your passions, and defining the impact you want to make. This process may take time and experimentation. Exploring different fields, volunteering, and reflecting on your experiences can help clarify your purpose. Remember, your "why" can evolve as you learn and grow.

2. **Embracing the Detours:** Turning Setbacks into Stepping Stones

Setbacks are inevitable. Rejection, mistakes, and even outright failure are part of the process. Resilient professionals view these challenges not as defeats but as opportunities for learning and growth. Think of your career like a video game: Each challenge you overcome makes you stronger and better equipped for the next level. Reframing your thinking, developing a growth mindset, practicing self-compassion, and seeking support are key strategies for levelling up your resilience. Remember, many successful individuals have faced numerous setbacks. Their ability to bounce back, learn from their mistakes, and persevere is what sets them apart.

3. **The Power of Connection:** Building Your Tribe

In our hyper-connected world, building a strong professional network is more important than ever. Networking is about building genuine relationships with people who can support, inspire, and open doors to new opportunities. As digital natives, Gen Z has a unique advantage in online networking. However, the power of face-to-face interactions should not be underestimated. Attending industry events, joining professional organizations, and making an effort to connect in person are all valuable. Authenticity, offering value to others, consistency, and embracing diversity are crucial for building a strong and supportive tribe.

4. **Adapting and Evolving:** Thriving in a Constantly Changing World

The only constant is change. The skills in demand today may be obsolete tomorrow. Adaptability and the willingness to evolve are essential for success. Gen Z is well-equipped to handle change, having grown up in a world of rapid technological advancements. Embracing lifelong learning, cultivating curiosity, developing adaptability, and staying informed about industry trends are crucial for staying ahead of the curve. Adapting and evolving is not just about surviving; it's about thriving.

5.　**Taking Care of Your Well-being:** The Foundation of Resilience

Resilience is not just about mental toughness; it's also about physical and emotional well-being. Prioritizing your mental and physical health is not a luxury; it's a necessity. Prioritizing sleep, eating healthy, exercising regularly, practicing mindfulness, setting boundaries, and seeking professional help when needed are all essential aspects of self-care. Your well-being is your foundation. When you take care of yourself, you'll be better equipped to handle the challenges of your career and achieve your goals.

Resilience as a Lifelong Journey

Resilience flourishes within supportive environments. Strong social connections, self-compassion, and finding purpose in adversity are essential for bouncing forward. Effective leadership plays a vital role in nurturing resilience within teams and organizations. This journey is not a destination but a continuous evolution. As the Chinese proverb states, 'The gem cannot be polished without friction, nor man perfected without trials.' This underscores the fundamental truth that challenges and setbacks are not obstacles but rather the very forces that shape our character and refine our potential. By embracing change, learning from setbacks, and prioritizing well-being, Gen Z can not only survive but also thrive amidst life's inevitable challenges. It's about learning to dance in the rain, finding joy amidst the storms, and emerging stronger and more empowered. This entails building a life of purpose, connection, and lasting fulfillment. This journey demands constant self-reflection, a willingness to adapt, and the courage to embrace vulnerability. Recognizing setbacks as detours, not roadblocks, is crucial. Cultivating a growth mindset, believing in our ability to learn and evolve, and using all experiences, positive and negative, as fuel for personal and professional growth is key. Challenge those negative thoughts, maintain perspective, and leverage optimism through affirmations and visualizations. Ultimately, resilience is the key to unlocking our full potential and crafting a life that is both successful and profoundly meaningful. It's the capacity to rise stronger, repeatedly, emerging from each challenge with enhanced wisdom, strength, and compassion. This skill, honed with practice and intention, empowers us to navigate the complexities of the modern world with grace, confidence, and unwavering hope, knowing that every trial is a step toward our perfect selves.

Building Your Resilience Toolkit: Practical Strategies for Gen Z

Beyond the core principles, here are some actionable strategies Gen Z professionals can use to build their resilience toolkit.

Goal Setting with Realistic Expectations: Start by breaking down your large goals into smaller, achievable steps. This approach fosters a sense of accomplishment and prevents you from feeling overwhelmed. Remember, being kind to yourself and avoiding unrealistic expectations can prevent disappointment and promote steady progress.

Embracing Adaptability and Flexibility: In today's rapidly changing world, being open to change and willing to adjust your plans is crucial. The ability to adapt with ease is a hallmark of resilience.

Boosting Self-Esteem: Recognize your strengths and celebrate your achievements, no matter how small. Focus on what you do well and build on those strengths. Embrace both your strengths and weaknesses, as understanding and accepting them is crucial.

Learning from Mistakes: Mistakes are inevitable—don't dwell on them. Instead, analyse what went wrong and identify lessons learned. This turns mistakes into valuable learning opportunities, allowing you to grow.

Developing Healthy Coping Mechanisms: Identify healthy ways to manage stress, such as exercise, hobbies, spending time with loved ones, or practicing relaxation techniques. Avoid unhealthy coping mechanisms like substance abuse or social withdrawal.

Cultivating Social Skills: Strong social skills are essential for building positive relationships and seeking assistance when needed. Practice active listening, empathy, and clear communication. Develop a robust social network, and don't hesitate to ask for help when you need it.

Practicing Self-Compassion: Be kind to yourself, especially during challenging times. Treat yourself with the same compassion you would offer a friend. Forgive yourself for your mistakes and understand that it's okay to be imperfect.

Honing Problem-Solving Skills: Develop your ability to analyse problems, brainstorm solutions, and implement effective strategies. Practice problem-solving in everyday situations to build your confidence.

Understanding and Accepting Emotions: Develop emotional intelligence by recognizing your own emotions and those of others. This awareness allows for better communication and stronger relationships. Pay attention to your feelings and accept them without judgment.

Adopting Optimistic Thinking Patterns: Focus on the positive aspects of situations and believe in your ability to overcome difficulties. Challenge negative thoughts and reframe them in a more positive light. Embracing optimism is key to resilient thinking.

Maintaining Balance: Balance different areas of your life, including work, relationships, hobbies, and personal time. This balance prevents burnout and promotes overall well-being.

Aligning with Values: Live and work in accordance with your core values. This alignment provides a sense of purpose and direction, which strengthens resilience.

Never Giving Up: Persistence is key. Don't give up on your goals, even when faced with setbacks. Learn from difficult situations and keep moving forward with determination.

Taking Risks: Don't be afraid to step outside your comfort zone and take calculated risks. This can lead to new opportunities and personal growth.

Spending Time Reflecting: Regularly reflect on your experiences, both positive and negative. This reflection helps you learn and grow from every situation.

Working on Your Strengths: Identify your strengths and focus on developing them further. Building on your strengths boosts confidence and enhances your ability to succeed.

Figure: The practical strategies to build your resilience:

The Power of Perspective and Reframing

Two powerful techniques for building resilience are perspective and reframing. Perspective helps you assess the true severity of a situation. Is it really a life-or-death matter? Often, things are not as dire as they initially seem. Reframing involves turning negative thoughts into positive ones. For example, a missed job opportunity can be reframed as a chance to explore other career paths.

Building a Resilient Future

Ultimately, resilience is the key to unlocking our full potential and crafting a life that is both successful and profoundly meaningful. It's the capacity to rise stronger, repeatedly, emerging from each challenge with enhanced wisdom, strength, and compassion. As Thomas Edison famously said, 'I have not failed. I've just found 10,000 ways that won't work.' This perspective encapsulates the essence of resilience: viewing setbacks not as failures but as invaluable learning experiences. This skill, honed with practice and intention, empowers us to navigate the complexities of the modern world with grace, confidence, and unwavering hope. By embracing these strategies and principles, Gen Z can cultivate a foundation of resilience, empowering them to thrive in the face of any challenge, understanding that every 'failure' is simply a step closer to success.

Actionable Exercises:

1. **The Resilience Reflection:** Think about a recent setback you had. Write down what happened, how you reacted initially, what emotions you felt, what you learned, and what you could do differently next time. Look for patterns in how you handle setbacks and try to develop a more positive, solution-focused approach.

2. **Setback to Strength:** Choose a past setback that really bothered you. Break it down into three parts: the challenge, your response at the time, and what you learned. Now, think about how you can use that lesson in a current or future challenge to make it a source of strength.

3. **The Resilience Journal:** Start a journal specifically for building resilience. Every day, write about a setback you faced, big or small, and how you dealt with it. Include what you could improve next time. At the end of each week, review

your entries and look for patterns. Over time, this journal will help you create a set of strategies for resilience.

4. **The 3-Step Rebound Plan:** When you face a setback, follow these three steps: first, pause and take a moment to process your emotions; second, reframe the situation by looking at it from a different perspective and asking what you can learn; and third, rebound by taking action based on what you've learned and setting a small, achievable goal to move forward.

5. **Support System Check-In:** Remember that resilience is stronger with support. Identify three people in your life who can offer guidance, encouragement, or advice during tough times. Reach out to them regularly, not just when you're struggling, to keep your support network strong.

Key Takeaways:

1. **Reframing Failure:** View setbacks as learning opportunities rather than personal failings.

2. **Cultivating Mental Fitness:** Practice mindfulness, meditation, and journaling to manage stress effectively.

3. **Gratitude and Reflection:** Use gratitude and reflection to build emotional strength and self-awareness.

4. **The Power of Support Systems:** Build strong networks of mentors, peers, and communities for support.

5. **Mental Agility:** Develop the ability to adapt and pivot in the face of uncertainty.

6. **Self-Care is Essential:** Prioritize physical, mental, and emotional well-being to build resilience.

7. **Grit Matters:** Combine passion and perseverance to achieve long-term goals.

8. **Stoic Approach:** Use perception, action, and will turn adversity into strength.

9. **Bouncing Forward:** Evolve through hardship and find new opportunities for growth.

10. **Resilience is a Lifelong Journey:** Continuously adapt, learn, and prioritize well-being to thrive.

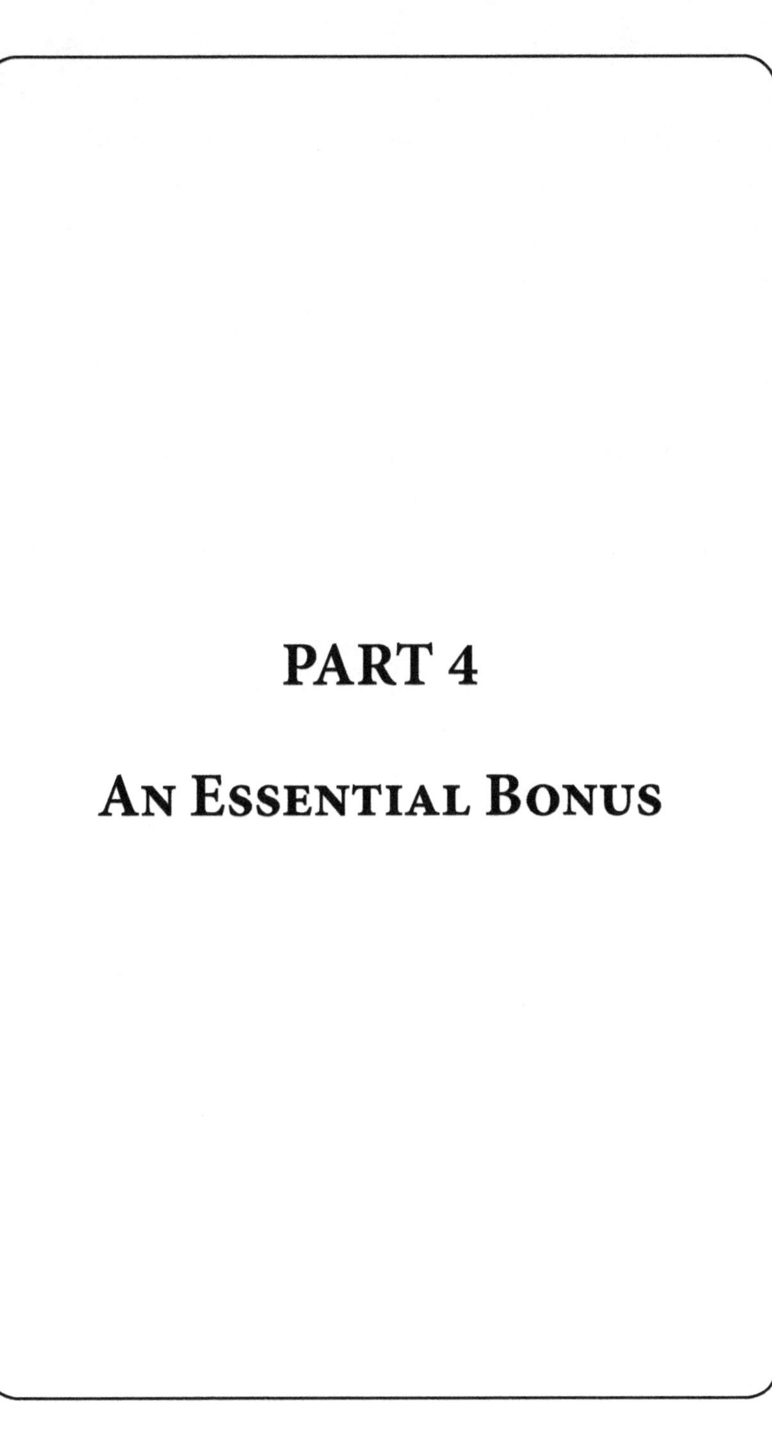

PART 4

AN ESSENTIAL BONUS

Chapter 10

NETWORKING IN A HYPERCONNECTED AGE: THE NEW RULES FOR BUILDING RELATIONSHIPS

The world has fundamentally shifted. Gone are the days of rigid networking events and obligatory handshakes. In today's hyperconnected era, building a powerful network transcends the mere collection of business cards and delves into the cultivation of authentic relationships. For Gen Z, digital natives at home in the online sphere, networking has evolved into a dynamic landscape of boundless opportunities. As the saying goes, 'It's not what you know, it's who you know.' While knowledge remains crucial, the ability to connect and collaborate with others is paramount in today's interconnected world. This chapter serves as your essential guide to navigating this new terrain, mastering the art of digital engagement, and building a network that will not only support but actively propel you toward your aspirations.

The Evolution of Networking: From Transactional to Transformative

Remember those stories your parents talked about networking? The endless conferences, the awkward small talk, the desperate attempts to impress someone important? Yeah, forget all that.

The old rules of networking – where it was all about "what can you do for me?" – simply don't work anymore. Gen Z values authenticity, transparency, and genuine connection. You're not interested in superficial interactions; you want to build relationships with people who share your values, understand your passions, and appreciate your unique perspective.

This shift is largely thanks to technology. Social media platforms like LinkedIn, Instagram, and X (Twitter) have revolutionized how we connect, offering a space where professionals can engage across geographical boundaries. While face-to-face interactions still hold value, the digital realm has become the primary arena for Gen Z to forge meaningful connections.

Building Your Personal Brand: Your Digital Identity

In a world saturated with information, standing out is crucial. This is where your personal brand comes in. Think of it as your unique digital fingerprint – a blend of your skills, experiences, and values that sets you apart from the crowd.

Your online presence is often the first impression you make, so be intentional about the image you project. Craft a compelling LinkedIn profile that showcases your achievements and aspirations. Curate your social media feeds to reflect your interests and expertise. Share your thoughts, insights, and experiences with the world.

Remember, building a personal brand is not about self-promotion; it's about showcasing your authentic self and the value you bring to the table.

Mastering the Art of Digital Engagement

As digital natives, Gen Z has a unique advantage in the networking arena. You've grown up with technology, seamlessly navigating social media platforms and online communities. This digital fluency is your superpower.

But digital engagement is more than just sending connection requests and accumulating followers. It's about actively participating in online conversations, sharing valuable content, and building relationships with people who resonate with your ideas.

Think of your online interactions as a form of "digital body language." Every comment, every share, and every like contribute to the impression you make. Be authentic, be respectful, and be engaging. Your digital footprint is your calling card, so make sure it reflects the best version of you.

The Niche Community Builder

Take the case of Divya, a Gen Z environmental science student with a passion for sustainable urban farming. She understood that simply having an Instagram account wasn't enough. Instead, she chose to actively cultivate a niche digital community.

Divya began by creating short, visually engaging videos demonstrating her own small-scale urban gardening techniques. She didn't just showcase her successes; she also shared her challenges and learning experiences, fostering an atmosphere of transparency and relatability.

She actively participated in relevant online forums and Twitter threads, offering thoughtful insights and answering questions about sustainable agriculture. She didn't just promote her own content; she also amplified the work of other environmental advocates, demonstrating a genuine interest in the broader community.

Divya's 'digital body language' was consistently positive and helpful. She responded to comments and direct messages promptly, engaging in genuine conversations. She also created a dedicated Discord server for urban farming enthusiasts, providing a space for real-time discussions and collaborative projects.

Over time, Divya's authentic engagement and valuable content attracted a dedicated following of like-minded individuals. She became known as a trusted voice in the sustainable urban farming community. This digital reputation led to real-world opportunities: invitations to speak at local sustainability events, collaborations with urban farms, and even a part-time role as a social media consultant for an environmental non-profit.

Divya's success wasn't about accumulating followers or chasing viral content. It was about consistently providing value, fostering genuine connections, and building a community around her passion. Her digital footprint became a testament to her expertise and commitment, opening doors to meaningful opportunities.

The Power of Community: Finding Your Tribe

Networking is not just about individual connections; it's about finding your community – a group of like-minded individuals who support you, challenge you, and inspire you to grow.

Online communities, forums, and groups offer a fantastic way to connect with people who share your interests and passions. Engage in discussions, share your expertise, and learn from others. These communities can become a valuable source of support, collaboration, and inspiration.

Remember, quality trumps quantity when it comes to building a strong network. Focus on cultivating deep, meaningful connections with people who genuinely understand and appreciate you. These are the relationships that will have a lasting impact on your life and career.

Giving Back: The Key to Reciprocity

Gen Z understands the power of collaboration and mutual support. You know that giving is just as important as receiving. This principle of reciprocity is fundamental to building a strong network.

When you generously offer your time, knowledge, and support to others, they are more likely to reciprocate. This doesn't mean keeping score or expecting immediate returns. It's about fostering a culture of generosity and mutual support within your network.

Think about how you can add value to the lives of the people you connect with. Can you offer your skills to help with a project? Can you share a valuable resource or make a helpful introduction? The more you give, the stronger your network will become.

The Power of Generous Contribution

Ali, a recent graphic design graduate, faced the challenge of breaking into a competitive freelance market. Instead of traditional cold outreach, he embraced a strategy of generous contribution.

He actively participated in an online community for small business owners, sharing his expertise freely. Ali created concise design tutorials, offered insightful branding advice, and even volunteered to redesign a local bakery's logo, asking for nothing in return.

His consistent generosity established him as a valuable and trusted resource. Community members began seeking his services, not just advice. Within six months, Ali's commitment to giving first resulted in a booming freelance business built entirely on referrals.

Crucially, one of his most significant clients stemmed directly from his initial act of goodwill. The bakery owner, deeply appreciative, recommended Ali to her brother, who led a national food chain.

Embrace Lifelong Learning: Stay Ahead of the Curve

In today's rapidly evolving world, continuous learning is no longer optional; it's essential. New technologies emerge constantly, industries transform, and the skills that are in demand today may be obsolete tomorrow.

Gen Z is known for its adaptability and eagerness to learn. Embrace this strength and make lifelong learning a priority. Attend workshops, take online courses, read industry publications, and engage in discussions with experts. The more you learn, the more valuable you become to your network, and the more opportunities will come your way.

Prioritizing Well-Being: Networking with Balance

Building and maintaining a strong network requires time, energy, and emotional investment. It's crucial to prioritize your well-being to avoid burnout.

Remember, you can't pour from an empty cup. Ensure you're getting enough sleep, eating healthy, and exercising regularly. Take breaks from technology, spend time in nature, and practice mindfulness to manage stress. Don't hesitate to ask for help when you need it.

Your well-being is the foundation for everything you do. When you take care of yourself, you'll be better equipped to build and nurture your network.

The Power of In-Person Connections: Don't Forget the Real World

While digital networking dominates the modern landscape, don't underestimate the power of in-person interactions. Face-to-face meetings create a deeper level of connection and trust that's hard to replicate online.

Make an effort to attend industry events, join professional organizations, and volunteer for causes you care about. These experiences provide valuable opportunities to meet new people, strengthen existing relationships, and build your network in a more personal way.

The In-Person Coffee That Opened Doors

Leila, a junior data analyst, admired a senior executive at her dream company, drawn to their insightful posts on industry trends. Instead of limiting their connection to LinkedIn, Leila took a bolder step.

She sent a personalized message proposing an in-person coffee meeting: 'Hi, I've been following your posts on AI trends and really admire your insights. Would you be open to meeting for coffee sometime? I'd love to learn more about your career journey and share my own aspirations.'

The executive agreed. During their face-to-face conversation, Leila's genuine curiosity and enthusiasm shone through. She asked thoughtful questions and shared her passion for data analysis. The executive was impressed.

'Your energy and drive are remarkable,' the executive said. 'Let's keep in touch. I'd be happy to introduce you to our data science team.'

Following their meeting, Leila received an invitation for an interview and, soon after, secured a position at the company. Their connection deepened into a valuable mentorship built on the foundation of their initial in-person interaction.

Networking for Introverts: Finding Your Style

Networking can feel intimidating, especially for introverts. But remember, you don't have to be the life of the party to build a strong network.

Focus on quality over quantity. Instead of trying to work a room full of strangers, prioritize meaningful conversations with a few individuals. Prepare beforehand by having a few conversation starters ready and setting realistic goals for the event.

Remember, networking is about building genuine connections, not putting on a performance. Be yourself, listen actively, and focus on building rapport. You'll be surprised at how fulfilling and effective this approach can be.

Nurturing Your Network: Building Relationships That Last

Building a network is not a one-time event; it's an ongoing process. Once you've made a connection, nurture that relationship through regular communication and engagement.

Follow up after meeting someone new, whether it's a quick thank-you note or a more detailed email. Stay in touch through social media, share relevant articles, and offer support when you can.

Remember, networking is about building relationships, not just collecting contacts. Invest time and effort in nurturing your connections, and they will become a valuable asset in your personal and professional life.

Networking: A Long-Term Investment in Your Future

Networking is not just a buzzword; it's a vital skill for navigating the modern world. It's an investment in your personal and professional growth that will pay dividends for years to come.

The connections you make today may not lead to immediate opportunities, but with consistent effort and genuine care, they will blossom into valuable relationships that support your journey.

Embrace the new rules of networking, prioritize authenticity and generosity, and watch your network become a powerful force for positive change in your life.

In today's hyperconnected world, networking isn't about collecting business cards; it's about cultivating genuine relationships. It's less about what someone can do for you *right now* and more about building a network of mutually beneficial connections that can blossom over time. So, how do you navigate this new landscape and build a thriving network?

Focus on Genuine Connection: The cornerstone of effective networking is authenticity. People can spot a transactional approach a mile away. Instead, approach every interaction with genuine curiosity. Be yourself – your unique personality is your greatest asset. Let your passion shine through but temper it with genuine interest in others. Focus on building rapport, not closing deals. Remember, the quality of your connections far outweighs the quantity.

Be a Generous Connector: One of the most powerful ways to strengthen your own network is to become a connector for others. Think about the people you meet and how their skills and experiences might complement each other. Introducing individuals who can benefit from knowing one another positions you as a valuable resource and strengthens the bonds within your network.

Prepare and Engage: Just like any important meeting, networking requires preparation. Research the companies and people you'd like to connect with. Have a mental list of talking points and thoughtful questions ready. Being prepared shows respect for the other person's time and allows for more meaningful conversations. When you're face-to-face, ask plenty of questions and truly listen to the answers. Attentive listening leaves a lasting impression. Remembering and using someone's name is a simple yet powerful way to show you value them.

Start Early, Stay Consistent: Don't wait until you're in a desperate situation to start networking. Building a strong network is a marathon, not a sprint. Start early and be consistent. Join local organizations, attend community events, and engage in online discussions. These activities provide opportunities to meet new people and nurture existing relationships.

Offer Value and Be a Resource: Become known as a valuable resource within your network. Share helpful articles, offer your expertise, and provide suggestions and ideas. Be clear about what you do and what makes you different. When you offer value freely and generously, people will naturally gravitate towards you.

Follow Up and Follow Through: After meeting someone new, gather their contact information and follow up promptly. A quick email or LinkedIn message saying you enjoyed meeting them can go a long way. If someone offers a referral, follow through quickly and efficiently. This demonstrates professionalism and strengthens trust.

Know What You Seek: While focusing on giving is crucial, it's also important to be able to articulate what you're looking for and how others might be able to help you. Being clear about your goals allows others to connect you with the right opportunities.

The Power of a Smile: Never underestimate the power of a genuine smile. It's a universal language that conveys warmth, friendliness, and approachability. A smile can make you more memorable and create a positive first impression.

In this hyperconnected age, networking transcends transactional exchanges; it's about cultivating genuine, mutually beneficial relationships. To build a thriving network that fuels your personal and professional growth, focus on authenticity, generosity, preparation, and consistent engagement. As Dale Carnegie wisely observed, 'You can make more friends in two months by becoming genuinely interested in other people than you can in two years by trying to get other people interested in you.' This principle underscores the importance of shifting the focus from self-promotion to genuine connection. By prioritizing active listening, understanding others' needs, and offering sincere support, you'll naturally attract meaningful relationships that will enrich your journey.

Figure: Networking tips

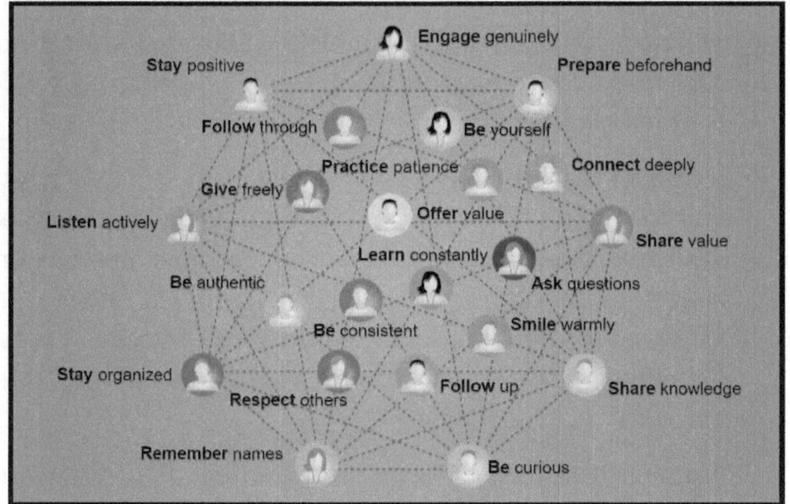

Actionable Exercises:

1. **Create Your Networking Map:** Take some time to visualize your current professional network. List the important people you know in different categories, like mentors, peers, or industry experts. Think about who's missing from your network, such as people from different industries or with different experiences. Over the next month, set a goal to reach out to at least three new people to grow your connections.

2. **Elevator Pitch Practice:** Write a short, 30-second summary of who you are, what you do, and what you're passionate about. Practice saying it naturally and confidently. Then, try it out in real conversations, whether at events, on video calls, or in casual meetings. Make it better based on feedback and practice until it feels authentic.

3. **The 5-Minute Connection:** Set a timer for five minutes each day and reach out to someone in your network with a brief,

personalized message. This could be a message on LinkedIn, a quick email, or a comment on social media. Focus on offering value by sharing something helpful, asking for their opinion, or congratulating them. Do this consistently for a week to build rapport.

4.   **Create a Follow-Up System:** After you meet someone new, whether online or in person, follow up with them within 24-48 hours. Send a quick thank-you message, mentioning something specific from your conversation to show you were paying attention. Add them to your contacts and set a reminder to reconnect in a few weeks. This will help you strengthen your relationships.

5.   **Host a Virtual Coffee Chat:** Set up a virtual coffee chat with someone you've connected with online but haven't spoken to yet. Prepare a few questions beforehand to make the conversation meaningful. Ask about their current projects, challenges, or thoughts on the industry. This is a great way to deepen connections and show genuine interest in others' work.

Key Takeaways:

1.   **Focus on Genuine Connection:** Prioritize building authentic relationships over transactional interactions.

2.   **Build Your Personal Brand:** Create a strong online presence that showcases your skills, experiences, and values.

3.   **Master Digital Engagement:** Actively participate in online conversations and share valuable content to build relationships.

4.   **Find Your Community:** Connect with like-minded individuals in online communities, forums, and groups.

5. **Give Back to Your Network:** Offer your time, knowledge, and support to others to foster reciprocity.

6. **Embrace Lifelong Learning:** Continuously learn and develop new skills to stay relevant and valuable.

7. **Prioritize Well-being:** Take care of your physical and mental health to effectively build and maintain your network.

8. **Don't Forget In-Person Connections:** Make an effort to attend events and meet people in person to create deeper connections.

9. **Networking is for Introverts Too:** Focus on quality over quantity and prioritize meaningful conversations.

10. **Nurture Your Network for the Long Term:** Invest time and effort in maintaining your connections to build valuable relationships.

YOUR BOLD FUTURE: CONCLUSION

As you step into the future, one thing is clear: Bold moves are no longer optional—they're essential. The world doesn't just need skilled professionals; it needs thinkers, doers, and leaders who redefine what's possible. You've explored the soft skills that will set you apart, but remember, knowledge alone doesn't create change. Action does.

Now is your moment to apply everything you've learned—to step forward, not just with confidence but with purpose. Let the insights from this book fuel your ambition, let the exercises sharpen your edge, and let your vision for the future drive you to take bold, intentional steps every day.

The path ahead won't always be easy. You'll face challenges, setbacks, and moments of doubt. But it's in those moments that your adaptability, resilience, and emotional intelligence will shine. It's there that your storytelling, collaboration, and ability to connect will become your superpowers. Each step you take will not only transform your career but also inspire others to follow your lead.

So, here's your challenge: What bold move will you make today? Will you start a conversation that matters, seize an opportunity that scares you, or commit to a habit that elevates your potential? Whatever it is, start now. Your bold future is waiting—not as a distant dream but as a series of intentional actions you choose to take.

Remember, the world is watching, but more importantly, you are. Make bold moves that align with your values, reflect your unique voice, and leave a legacy that matters. The future isn't just happening—it's yours to create.

Let's get started.

BIBLIOGRAPHY

- Dhawan, Erica. *Digital Body Language: How to Lead Your Company's Culture by Leveraging the New Rules of Human Behavior Online*. St. Martin's Press, 2021.

- Clark, Dorie. *Reinventing You: Define Your Brand, Imagine Your Future*. Harvard Business Review Press, 2013.

- Headlee, Celeste. *We Need to Talk: How to Have Conversations That Matter*. Harper One, 2017.

- Gallo, Carmine. *Talk Like TED: The 9 Public-Speaking Secrets of the World's Top Minds*. St. Martin's Press, 2014.

- Coyle, Daniel. *The Culture Code: The Secrets of Highly Successful Groups*. Bantam Books, 2018.

- Rushkoff, Douglas. *Program or Be Programmed: Ten Commands for a Digital Age*. OR Books, 2010.

- Andrews, Gill. *Making Your Website Work: 100 Copy & Design Tweaks for Smart Business Owners*. CreateSpace Independent Publishing Platform, 2017.

- Wong, Dona M. *The Wall Street Journal Guide to Information Graphics: The Dos and Don'ts of Presenting Data, Facts, and Figures*. Pearson Education, 2010.

- Handley, Ann. *Everybody Writes: Your Go-To Guide to Creating Ridiculously Good Content*. Wiley, 2014.

- Gallager, Robert G. *Principles of Digital Communication*. Cambridge University Press, 2008.

- Krogerus, Mikael, and Roman Tshappeler. *The Communication Book*. Perigee Books, 2017.

- Vaynerchuk, Gary. *Crush It!: Why NOW Is the Time to Cash In on Your Passion*. HarperStudio, 2009.

- Schawbel, Dan. *Me 2.0: 4 Steps to Building Your Future*. Kaplan Publishing, 2009.

- McLaughlin, Justin. *The Personal Brand Blueprint: A No-Nonsense Guide to Personal Branding*. Career Press, 2016.

- Kleon, Austin. *Show Your Work!: 10 Ways to Share Your Creativity and Get Discovered*. Workman Publishing, 2014.

- Clark, Dorie. *Stand Out: How to Find Your Breakthrough Idea and Build a Following Around It*. Portfolio, 2015.

- Scott, David Meerman. *The Personal Branding Playbook: Actionable Strategies for Creating a Unique Professional Identity*. Wiley, 2017.

- McNally, David, and Karl Speak. *The Brand You 50: Fifty Ways to Transform Yourself from an Ordinary Person into a Brand*. Hachette Books, 2008.

- Kaufman, Josh. *The Personal MBA: Master the Art of Business*. Penguin Books, 2010.

- Sivers, Derek. *The Power of Starting Something Stupid: How to Crush Bad Ideas and Save Your Business*. Penguin Books, 2011.

- Kawasaki, Guy, and Peg Fitzpatrick. *The Art of Social Media: Power Tips for Power Users*. Penguin Books, 2014.

- Neumeier, Marty. *The Brand Gap: How to Bridge the Distance Between Business Strategy and Design*. New Riders, 2003.

- Heath, Chip, and Dan Heath. *Made to Stick: Why Some Ideas Survive and Others Die*. Random House, 2007.

- Gottschall, Jonathan. *The Storytelling Animal: How Stories Make Us Human*. Houghton Mifflin Harcourt, 2012.

◆ Dicks, Matthew. *Storyworthy: Engage, Teach, Persuade, and Change Your Life through the Power of Storytelling*. St. Martin's Press, 2019.

◆ Olson, Randy. *The Narrative Gym: Introducing the ABT Framework for Messaging and Communication*. Narrative Science, 2015.

◆ Miller, Donald. *Building a StoryBrand: Clarify Your Message So Customers Will Listen*. HarperCollins, 2017.

◆ Storr, Will. *The Science of Storytelling: Why Stories Make Us Human and How to Tell Them Better*. St. Martin's Press, 2019.

◆ Cialdini, Robert. *Influence: The Psychology of Persuasion*. HarperCollins, 1984.

◆ Duarte, Nancy. *Resonate: Present Visual Stories that Transform Audiences*. Wiley, 2010.

◆ Quesenbery, Whitney, and Kevin Brooks. *Storytelling for User Experience: Crafting Stories for Better Design*. Rosenfeld Media, 2010.

◆ Walsh, John D. *The Art of Storytelling: Easy Steps to Presenting an Unforgettable Story*. Greenleaf Book Group Press, 2011.

◆ Bradberry, Travis, and Jean Greaves. *Emotional Intelligence 2.0*. TalentSmart, 2009.

◆ Stein, Steven J., and Howard E. Book. *The EQ Edge: Emotional Intelligence and Your Success*. Wiley, 2011.

◆ Meyer, Erin. *The Culture Map: Breaking Through the Invisible Boundaries of Global Business*. PublicAffairs, 2014.

◆ Davis, Shirley. *Diversity, Equity & Inclusion for Dummies*. Wiley, 2021.

◆ Auger-Domínguez, Daisy. *Inclusion Revolution: The Essential Guide to Dismantling Racial Inequity in the Workplace*. Harper Business, 2021.

- Goleman, Daniel, Richard Boyatzis, and Annie McKee. *Primal Leadership: Unleashing the Power of Emotional Intelligence.* Harvard Business Review Press, 2002.

- Brown, Brené. *Dare to Lead: Brave Work. Tough Conversations. Whole Hearts.* Random House, 2018.

- Brackett, Marc. *Permission to Feel: Unlocking the Power of Emotions to Help Our Kids, Ourselves, and Our Society Thrive.* Celadon Books, 2019.

- Lynn, Adele B. *The EQ Difference: A Powerful Plan for Putting Emotional Intelligence to Work.* Career Press, 2009.

- Pollak, Lindsey. *The Remix: How to Lead and Succeed in the Multigenerational Workplace.* McGraw-Hill, 2019.

- Koulopoulos, Thomas, and Dan Keldsen. *The Gen Z Effect: Applying Gen Z Insights to the Workplace, Markets, and World.* Bibliomotion, 2014.

- Elmore, Tim, and Andrew McPeak. *Unfiltered: Gen Z, Social Media, and the Inside-Out Revolution.* Re-Thinking, 2021.

- Jay, Meg. *The Defining Decade: Why Your Twenties Matter—And How to Make the Most of Them Now.* Twelve, 2012.

- Perna, Dr. Mark C. *The Gen Z Leader: How to Engage and Empower the Generation that Will Change Everything.* Routledge, 2020.

- McGowan, Heather E., and Chris Shipley. *The Adaptation Advantage: Let Go, Learn Fast, and Thrive in the Future of Work.* Wiley, 2020.

- Jenkins, Ryan. *The Generation Z Guide: The Complete Manual to Understand, Recruit and Lead the Next Generation.* 2020.

- Marquet, L. David. *Leadership is Language: The Hidden Power of What You Say and What You Don't.* Portfolio, 2020.

- Harvard Business Review. *HBR Guide to Leading Teams.* Harvard Business Review Press, 2019.

- Heath, Chip, and Dan Heath. *The Power of Moments: Why Certain Experiences Have Extraordinary Impact.* Simon & Schuster, 2018.

- Fried, Jason, and David Heinemeier Hansson. *Remote: Office Not Required.* Crown Business, 2013.

- Dhar, Julia, and Jennifer Moss. *The Hybrid Work Handbook: How to Thrive in the New World of Work.* HarperCollins, 2021.

- Sutherland, Lisette. *Work Together Anywhere: A Handbook for Globally Distributed Teams.* O'Reilly Media, 2020.

- Raman, Venu. *The Collaboration Economy: How to Find Success in an Interconnected World.* CreateSpace Independent Publishing Platform, 2018.

- Olson, Judy, and Gary Olson. *Working Together Apart: Collaboration over the Internet.* Oxford University Press, 2000.

- Pullan, Penny. *Virtual Leadership: Practical Strategies for Getting the Best Out of Virtual Work and Virtual Teams.* Wiley, 2016.

- Dhawan, Erica. *Digital Body Language: How to Build Trust & Connection, No Matter the Distance.* St. Martin's Press, 2021.

- Newport, Cal. *Deep Work: Rules for Focused Success in a Distracted World.* Grand Central Publishing, 2016.

- Eyal, Nir. *Indistractable: How to Control Your Attention and Choose Your Life.* BenBella Books, 2019.

- Bailey, Chris. *Hyperfocus: How to Be More Productive in a World of Distraction.* Viking, 2018.

- Knapp, Jake, and John Zeratsky. *Make Time: How to Focus on What Matters Every Day.* Bantam, 2018.

- Ferriss, Timothy. *The 4-Hour Workweek: Escape 9-to-5, Live Anywhere, and Join the New Rich.* Crown Publishing, 2007.

- Allen, David. *Getting Things Done: The Art of Stress-Free Productivity*. Penguin Books, 2001.

- Tracy, Brian. *Eat That Frog!: 21 Great Ways to Stop Procrastinating and Get More Done in Less Time*. Berrett-Koehler Publishers, 2001.

- Clear, James. *Atomic Habits: An Easy & Proven Way to Build Good Habits & Break Bad Ones*. Avery, 2018.

- Covey, Stephen R. *The 7 Habits of Highly Effective People*. Free Press, 1989.

- McKeown, Greg. *Essentialism: The Disciplined Pursuit of Less*. Crown Business, 2014.

- Epstein, David. *Range: Why Generalists Triumph in a Specialized World*. Riverhead Books, 2019.

- Roose, Kevin. *Futureproof: 9 Rules for Humans in the Age of Automation*. Penguin Press, 2021.

- Taleb, Nassim Nicholas. *Antifragile: Things That Gain from Disorder*. Random House, 2012.

- Broza, Gil. *The Agile Mindset: Making Agile Processes Work*. Lean Agility, 2012.

- Johnson, Spencer. *Who Moved My Cheese?* Putnam Publishing Group, 1998.

- Heath, Chip, and Dan Heath. *Switch: How to Change Things When Change Is Hard*. Broadway Books, 2010.

- Ryan, M.J. *Adaptability: How to Survive Change You Didn't Ask For*. Berrett-Koehler Publishers, 2018.

- McGowan, Heather E. *The Adaptation Advantage: Let Go, Learn Fast, and Thrive in the Future of Work*. Wiley, 2020.

- Duhigg, Charles. *The Power of Habit: Why We Do What We Do in Life and Business*. Random House, 2012.

◆ Duckworth, Angela. *Grit: The Power of Passion and Perseverance*. Scribner, 2016.

◆ Holiday, Ryan. *The Obstacle Is the Way: The Timeless Art of Turning Trials into Triumph*. Portfolio, 2014.

◆ Sandberg, Sheryl, and Adam Grant. *Option B: Facing Adversity, Building Resilience, and Finding Joy*. Knopf, 2017.

◆ Brooks, Robert, and Sam Goldstein. *The Power of Resilience: Achieving Balance, Confidence, and Personal Strength in Your Life*. McGraw-Hill, 2004.

◆ Brown, Brené. *Rising Strong*. Random House, 2015.

◆ Frankl, Viktor E. *Man's Search for Meaning*. Beacon Press, 2006.

◆ Westover, Tara. *Educated: A Memoir*. Random House, 2018.

◆ Strayed, Cheryl. *Wild: From Lost to Found on the Pacific Crest Trail*. Alfred A. Knopf, 2012.

◆ van der Kolk, Bessel. *The Body Keeps the Score: Brain, Mind, and Body in the Healing of Trauma*. Viking, 2014.

◆ Kingsley, Theodore. *Networking Skills: 3-in-1 Guide to Master Business Networking, Personal Social Network & Networking for Introverts*. 2023.

◆ Harvard Business Review. *HBR Guide to Smarter Networking*. Harvard Business Review Press, 2022.

◆ Bridges, Beth, and Bob Burg. *Networking on Purpose: A Five-Part Success Plan to Build a Powerful and Profitable Business Network*. Wiley, 2015.

◆ Darling, Diane. *The Networking Survival Guide, Second Edition: Practical Advice to Help You Gain Confidence, Approach People, and Get the Success You Want*. McGraw-Hill, 2010.

◆ Dr. Malika Nanda, Bonding with GenZ @ Work: Attract & Retain Talent and Generate Advocacy for your Brand, 2024.

- Fisher, David J.P. *Networking in the 21ˢᵗ Century... on LinkedIn: Creating Online Relationships and Opportunities.* 2020.

- Edelman, Richard, and Michael J. Silverstein. *Superconnector: Stop Networking and Start Building Genuine Relationships.* Harper Business, 2020.

- Dhawan, Erica. *Digital Body Language: How to Build Trust & Connection in a Tech-First World.* St. Martin's Press, 2021.

- Hyatt, Michael. *Platform: Get Noticed in a Noisy World.* Thomas Nelson, 2012.

- Grant, Adam. *Give and Take: Why Helping Others Drives Our Success.* Viking, 2013.

- Ferrazzi, Keith. *Never Eat Alone: And Other Secrets to Success, One Connection at a Time.* Crown Business, 2005.